Through Christ our Lord

Acknowledgements

The author and publishers gratefully acknowledge the following permissions to reproduce copyright material. All possible attempts have been made to contact copyright holders and to acknowledge their copyright correctly.

The Divine Office (from Vol. II, p.154–5: Sermon 43 of St Peter Chrysologus – and from Vol. III, p.585: Concluding Prayer for 26th Sunday of the Year) copyright 1974 by HarperCollins Ltd. *The Jerusalem Bible* (Is. 58:7,9, Mk. 15:34), published and copyright 1966, 1967 and 1968 by Darton, Longman and Todd Ltd and used by permission of the publishers. *The New Jerusalem Bible* (Gen. 4:1–16, Mt. 8:5–13, Mt. 11–25, Lk. 15:11–32), published and copyright 1985 by Darton, Longman and Todd Ltd and Doubleday & Co Inc, and used by permission of the publishers. *The Poems of Gerard Manley Hopkins* (4th edn. ed W H Gardner and N H Mackenzie, p.27), published and copyright 1967 by Oxford University Press and used by permission of the publishers. *The Psalms: a New Translation* (Ps. 21:14–15, Ps. 31:1–1, Ps. 68:4, Ps. 21:16, Ps. 40:4, Ps. 102:11–12) published by HarperCollins Ltd. *The Return of the Native* by Thomas Hardy, published by Macmillan General Books. *Revised Standard Version* of the Bible (details of the many references found within the text) published by Oxford University Press. *Death of a Son (who died in a mental hospital, aged one)* from Selected Poems by Jon Silkin, published 1994 by Sinclair-Stevenson and used with permission. *Surgical Ward* from W H Auden: A Selection by the Author, published by Penguin Books Ltd.

Through Christ our Lord

Gerard Mackrell

First published in 1996

Gracewing
Fowler Wright Books
2 Southern Ave, Leominster
Herefordshire HR6 0QF

ISBN 0 85244 301 3

Typesetting by
Action Typesetting Ltd, Gloucester, GL1 1SP

Printed by Redwood Books
Trowbridge, Wiltshire, BA14 8RN

Contents

Contents

Introduction

The meditations that follow illustrate different situations of prayer, the majority of them taken from the New Testament. The situations of the prayers, the moods of those who pray, are different from one another, but all have one thing in common which is central to the nature of prayer: the prayers come from what the pray-ers think and feel at the time of the prayer, not from the feelings they think they should have. The prayers flow naturally from the experiences and feelings which exist immediately before these feelings are uttered in prayer. For prayer is utterance; the outering of what is within us; the uttering of Us. In a sense we are our prayer, and our prayer is us. The definition of prayer as 'a raising of the mind and heart to God' is accurate as long as the 'mind and heart' that is 'raised' really is what we feel and think. Otherwise it cannot be 'raised'. If Cain did not pray his anger – and he did not – he did not 'raise' it to God; and so could not purge it. His feelings there found another outlet – murder. If Jesus had not screamed his cry of dereliction on the Cross he could not, as man, have found comfort. If the tax-collector in the Temple, in Luke's parable, had not bared his tormented guilt-ridden soul to God he could never have been drowned in the torrent of divine forgiveness.

If we desperately feel the need to pray *we are in the process of praying*. Prayer is communication that leads to communion, but often the communication is a struggle. In prayer we may simply have to pray about our inability or unwillingness to pray; about what we feel at the moment rather than about what we think we *should* feel. By such uncompromising communications will we achieve communion, but only by speaking our minds, which may mean howling or whining, rather than singing God's praises. There must be no question of 'faking' a mood of well-being in prayer while actually toying with the idea of suicide. We may well have to put on a brave face to others – but not to God. Our prayer, like that of the psalmist, may be 'from out of the depths' of what seems totally inescapable torment. And our prayers, like those of the poet Hopkins, may seem to bounce off 'a brazen heaven' and echo mockingly back at us. The apparent serenity of others may aggravate rather than alleviate this miserable situation. Or we may think that we are not *good* enough to pray, which can really mean that we think that prayer is not good enough for *us*, that it is inadequate to our needs, something to do only *after* we have solved our outstanding problems. Indeed, *not* to pray may seem to be the brave and stoical thing to do, which means that we are seeking a solution within ourselves; and there isn't one.

In the psalms, those of lament bring us the greatest comfort, precisely because they seem to lack it – not comfort in the Aristotelian sense of 'catharsis,' cleansing us from our own fear by pity and fear for fictional people, but comfort in the sense that the psalms express real states of mind – even though the expression of these states of mind is sometimes exaggerated in its imagery. If we read these psalms, or simply stare numbly at them, we are praying, for the suffering itself is the prayer. The musical instrument in these psalms is not the harp, but the harpist; the singer, not the song. Nerves are taut; resonating when God plucks at them. His skin is stretched tightly over his bones; providing the greater resonance when God's drumsticks beat. Such apparently discordant sounds echo most melodiously simply because they are sounds of prayer.

Stick a pin in someone and you will elicit a response, even if it is a sock on the jaw. In the psalms God does not stop at pin-pricks of course, but it is not a wilful or malicious God we are dealing with. He does not have to prove to *himself* that we are alive; he often has to prove it to *us*.

Suffering often seems to numb us. But even then we need to *say* and *pray* that we *are* numb, and then see what happens. The prayer *will* be answered, for the praying itself is part of the answer. 'Seek and you shall find' is really 'Seek, and you have already found' – by your very seeking. But, again, this is only if the prayer is absolutely sincere and as spontaneous as possible.

Psalm 44, for example, comes close to blasphemy when the psalmist more or less accuses God of breaking his covenant.

> 'You have made us the taunt of our neighbours,
> the derision and scorn of those about us.
> You have made us a byword among the nations,
> a laughing stock among the peoples ...
> ... All this has come upon us,
> though we have not forgotten *you*
> or been false to *your* covenant.
>
> (Ps. 43(44) 13–14, 17)

That is the kind of talk one might expect to draw fire down from heaven. But the psalmist is in no mood for reverential preliminaries. He knows the value of patient endurance, but he also knows his own limits! 'Lord, will you desert us for*ever*?' Enough is enough. Jesus himself taught us to pray: 'Lead us not into temptation,' which is really reminding ourselves – and prayer gives this reminder – that God 'will not tempt [test] us above that which we are able.'

At times like this the psalmist not only softens his accusation by drawing God's attention to his human weakness (including impulsiveness and loss of temper) but he also uses his weakness as a bargain tool. God will not push us too far 'for he knows of what we are made; he knows that we are but dust.'

Many of the psalms may disedify us by their whining, cursing, fuming, as well as their anger, self-pity, self-interest. Yet these disedifying psalms are a form of praise, and of the highest kind. To ask for help is to acknowledge the power to help of the one we ask. Not to ask may be an insult. To blame others is to recognise their responsibility; not to blame may be to deny them any control, even over events over which they *should* exercise control.

To ask is to praise. 'Give us this day our daily bread' is as much a prayer of praise as 'Hallowed be thy name.' No need to tell this to the psalmist, of course; he tells us. He blamed God as freely as he thanked him. God could not have it both ways; if he took the credit he took the blame. We may regard this as naïve or even blasphemous, and preen ourselves at being more understanding of the evil around us. But we may need to ask ourselves whether such an 'understanding' is in reality a failure to take God seriously.

The psalmist poured all his anger and bitterness into his prayer. For him prayer was not merely 'a raising of the mind and heart to God,' but a raising of the concrete mind and heart he had *at the moment of prayer.* He did not wait for the 'right dispositions' – whatever these may be! He prayer to receive the dispositions of calmness, peace, courage and insight.

The feelings of the psalmist were worked off *in* his prayer, which was a kind of poultice, sucking out the venom which festered inside him. He spoke to God as we speak to a doctor, a friend, at times an enemy. But he *spoke*. He did not pretend to be disinterested. He knew that his dependence was on God, not God's on him; and he *said* so and 'utterance' can take many forms.

In Jon Silkin's poem 'Death of a Son (who died in a mental hospital, aged one)', the child had never been able to utter a sound, betray an emotion, or show the slightest response to a father who strained every sense in the hope of catching some response – until the moment of the child's death:

> He turned over on his side with his one year
> Red as a wound
> He turned over as if he could be sorry for this;
> And out of his eyes two great tears rolled, like stones, and he died.

We can feel, never mind hear, the last great heave, as two big tears are forced out of his eyes, the only fruit of the little tree. And just in time. Before the baby's soul escapes from the body something escapes from the soul. He has finally uttered.

Often however the psalmist screamed and raved, and the covers of a Bible do not muffle those screams. The fact that we so effortlessly take such psalms as songs of praise – the meaning of the word 'psalm' – may in fact indicate that we take the psalmist no more seriously than we sometimes take God.

Even the prayer which seems to be 'pure praise' involves our own needs. Psalm 102 offers us an example of the adroit way in which the psalmist combines the two. At first his prayer seems to be a wistful reflection on human mortality, with more than a dash of self-pity. Until we note the deliberate contrast: '*My* days are like a passing shadow, and *I* wither away like grass. But *you*, O Lord, will endure forever, and *your* name from age to age.' The psalmist is not concerned here with death, but with stability during life; and God's eternity and unchangingness gives him this. He seeks firmness outside himself and in God, but he seeks it *for* himself. Take away human life and he can accept this; take away God and the psalmist's mind topples.

Nor is the psalmist above using his own weakness and mortality as his strength. Since 'our life is over like a sigh', and since our seventy or eighty years are 'full of emptiness and pain,' then God should 'relent.' This is the kind of artfulness Jesus praised in prayer when recounting the story of the woman who disturbed an unjust judge. He, too, spoke not so much of tapping fearfully at the doors of heaven, rather of tearing them off their hinges. For if we leave our real feelings out of prayer, we shall only sink back into them *after* prayer – if indeed, we can call what we have done prayer.

Praise of God in no way resembles the vicarious pleasure we may derive from watching the two dimensional antics of the brave and beautiful of Hollywood. 'Come *in*!' Let us bow and bend low; let us kneel before the God who made us' (Ps.95). For the God who made us is the God who still makes us, and who is responsible for his handiwork. He must be praised for making us – even us. To avoid this truth is to say that prayer is not for us.

Far from removing us from reality, then, prayer brings us closer to it; enabling us to face it and cope with it. There is little comfort in facing reality if we cannot cope.

The most 'real' part of reality is often experienced in suffering, since our awareness of things is never so sharp as when we fear them. In his poem 'The Surgical Ward,' W H Auden describes the plight of a man with a cancerous wound on his leg. For that man the whole reality is centred on the locus of plain: 'All the world lay beneath the bandage.'

In 'Fingers in the Door,' David Holbrook describes absent-mindedly catching his young daughter's fingers in the door jamb and watching helplessly while the child 'contorts herself foetus-wise against the burning fact of the pain.' Five lines on we read: 'The child's cry broke,' and we expel our own breath with relief at her scream. The expression of the pain of course provides some psychological relief, but does not remove the *fact* of the pain. The father clasps his daughter to him in a tight embrace, but no osmosis can transfer the child's pain to him. He is forced to conclude that we are all 'light-years away' from even those we love. The child contorts herself 'foetus-wise,' as we all fold up over the point of pain; in the more agonized psalms we are frequently faced with a refinement of anguish. We find the psalmist in pits and graves that effectively muffle his cries; or in swamps, deeps, and waters that always seem to be at mouth-level. Often the suffering comes from the sense of imprisonment created precisely by this inability to pray: 'Imprisoned, I cannot escape ... I am drowned beneath your waves' (Ps. 88). Yet he *does* escape, and lives to tell the tale – or the psalm.

That is prayer as us speaking to God. But it is also God speaking to us. Before we speak to him, God has spoken to us through us. Our very existence is God's speaking: God's speaking, not God's having spoken. God did not create us; he creates us. And his creating is his speaking. In another way God speaks first. When we receive forgiveness we should thank God for two graces, not one: for the grace of forgiveness, and for the grace to ask for it. God's prompting graces, his 'speaking', need not be mystical or mysterious; he will not write in blood on the ceiling, nor whisper in a dream. He works through us, through our bodies, through our temperaments, through our health, through our joy and hope and love, as well as through the painful opposites of all these. In the prophecy of Isaiah the Lord says through the prophet that what he wants is mercy and justice and love shown in very physical and earthbound ways, as opposed to empty non-earthbound 'prayers': '... share your bread with the hungry, and ... shelter the homeless poor ...' (Is. 58:7). Then, he says, God is near us, next to us, in us: 'Cry, and the Lord will answer; call, and he will say, "I am here"' (Is. 58:9). It is as if we shout aloud to someone we think is at the other side of a field and, to our surprise and shock, we hear that person whisper, 'I am here': at our side; and the nearness startles us.

Prayer of Listening

There are two great obstacles to prayer; God is either too far away, or much too close. At times we may say with the psalmist, 'My eyes are wasted away from looking for my God' (Ps.68(69):4); and at others (probably less frequently) we gasp, 'Who can see the face of the Lord and live?' This latter is the ultimate deterrent to prayer, yet Metropolitan Anthony of Sourozh sees the awesomeness of the encounter with the holiness of God as the very essence of prayer.* Awareness of the utter contrast between ourselves and God can, of course, suck us into prayer as well as deter us in our fear. At such times we may envy those who complain, 'I'm not getting anywhere in prayer', and wish that we could comfortably distance ourselves into a pleasant boredom rather than face that terrifying encounter. There may be times when we feel that the effrontery of writing about prayer is as nothing compared to the impertinence of actually praying; talking about prayer may seem less hypocritical than actually praying. For if I pray, rather than merely talk or write about it, I am faced with a God who is going to make uncomfortable demands upon me. That fear is already within me before I begin to encounter God in prayer, but it is precisely in prayer that it will be allayed: not because I discover that God will not make demands on me after all – he will! but because he will also talk to me about such demands, and assure me of his all-powerful help.

To be frightened of prayer at least shows that I take it seriously.

---

* See *Living Prayer* by Archbishop Antony Bloom (Darton, Longman and Todd, 1966), ch. 1. 'The Essence of Prayer'.

The reason I do not pray is because I know that I am unwilling to put my prayer into practice! We are all cowards and – to some extent at least – hypocrites. But even our possibly somewhat ambivalent attitude to prayer may be a gift from God as it at least shows that there is *some* contact between God and myself. We may well find that we have no peace until we tackle and resolve our fear of prayer.

Let us now consider the common experience of those who find prayer unprofitable because God seems too distant; there is no contact with him. As we have seen, this can also be a form of the fear of finding a God who is too close; we do not find him because, in our heart of hearts, we do not *wish* to find him. It is as if we have an inbuilt thermostat which switches off the relationship when it threatens to go deeper than the making of polite observations about the weather. But let us assume for the moment that God's apparent distance is something that we genuinely regret. (We are of course treating the symptoms rather than root causes.)

Prayer can feel like a one-way street. We do all the talking; God does not reply. He may hear, but we do not *hear* him hearing. We would even prefer to hear him saying No, rather than not hear him saying Yes. We seem either to be speaking into a void, or just whispering to ourselves. Our prayers either do not go far enough, or else they go too far and we cannot make out where they have got to. The Jesuit poet Gerard Manley Hopkins describes his prayers not getting through. They bounce off a brazen heaven and echo mockingly back at him with an empty metallic ring.

> My prayers must meet a brazen heaven
> And fail or scatter all away.*

At other times prayer seems to pierce an all too penetrable layer and disappear, dissipated in a vacuum: not unlike putting a letter into a bottle and throwing it into the sea. But it is not merely a question of praying for something specific which is not given, but of God's total silence; he does not even acknowledge receipt of the request. We feel as if we are talking to ourselves.

* *The Poems of Gerard Manley Hopkins*, 4th edn., ed. W.H. Gardner and N.H. Mackenzie (Oxford University Press 1967), no. 18. p. 27.

What do we mean when we say that we are 'not getting anywhere in prayer?' It is likely that we are looking for emotional reassurance, which we shall almost certainly fail to find; or else we are seeking a miracle. Not that we are necessarily conscious of wanting the miraculous; few would survive the 'Belshazzar experience' of seeing an amputated finger writing a message on the wall. But we would like a little bit more of what spiritual writers call 'consolations'. They come but seldom.

We are seeking – and are disappointed not to find – more 'body' in prayer; more mental involvement, more *feeling*. And yet it is precisely the 'body', in the fullest sense, which is fully engaged in that prayer which is apparently dry and empty; prayer devoid of the nice warm reassuring feeling. We feel that we are talking to ourselves: we are in fact talking *through* ourselves – to God; and God talks to us through us. It is an outward sign of the inner grace of God, and it started long before the Incarnation, when of course it took on a profound and sublime significance. God's communion with us, and ours with him, began when he breathed a soul into mud and called it man. Through body, brain, blood and bone we speak to God, and God to us. Even the most mystical of contacts with God comes through the body. Jesus told Peter that it was not 'flesh and blood' but the Father in heaven who revealed to him the Messiahship of Jesus; but it was *through* 'flesh and blood' that the Father revealed it. When we say that we do not *feel* God's presence in prayer we are speaking of the 'body'. It is as though we are expecting some extra-corporeal force to create a feeling that is of its nature corporeal. There is more to the 'body' than feeling.

When we say that we do not hear God answering us, speaking back, we make the understandable mistake of thinking that it is we who open the conversation in prayer. It is not. Who do we think gives us the power to pray, the desire to pray? No one can say 'Jesus is Lord' without the power of the Holy Spirit (I Cor. 12:3); nor can anyone say, 'Jesus is *not* Lord' without the God-given power to speak and think. God speaks to us in our very speaking to him. It is we who speak back, not God. At the root of our restlessness in prayer is our dissociation of prayer from life. We even speak of our 'prayer-life' as if it were distinct from the rest of 'life'. We go so far as to place it in a different category from the actions we regard as 'spiritual' such as being kind, patient, chaste (or their 'unspiritual' opposites.) 'Prayer life' can suggest a retreat from a world devoid of the ethereal atmosphere we think necessary for prayer. But prayer will only take place, if it takes place at all, in the world of things we bump our heads against. Fail to grasp this, and we shall never 'hear' God.

For example, I say to God, 'Lord, I love you. At least I want to. Or I want to want to love you.' That is God speaking *to* me *through* me. How else can he speak to me, short of a miracle? It is not a question of being 'practical' in the sense of 'no-nonsense about all this mystical stuff', but of a deep faith in God's creation. God did not *make* me; he *makes* me. Now. If he forgot me for a split second I would vanish as a dream vanishes when I awake. That creative act includes, of course, all that I do as well as all that I am. It is therefore God speaking to me through my being and my doing: through *me*, body and soul. So when we pray we should reverse the sequence of petitioning used with other people. Normally we say 'Please' first, and 'Thank You' after the request has been granted. In prayer it must be the other way round: 'Thank you, Lord, for giving me the grace to say "Please".' For every word we say, God says. Every heartbeat needs his permission.

When we seek an 'infused knowledge', or mind-to-mind contact with God, we are foolishly reaching for the angelic; the reality is that our human nature, body-soul, is enough for us. That is how God came to us, by creating us; that is how he came in the Incarnation. So our thinking, scratching our heads, crossing and uncrossing our legs, is not only *our* action, but our *God-given* action. It is not the prelude to prayer; it is the beginning of prayer – and it may well be the end of prayer, which is better than no prayer at all!

Prayer is in the cranking of the brain to ignite ideas: in that mysterious union of body and soul we need look for no further mystery. That is the point where God meets us. Do not listen for anything else! We know that God is Spirit, though the knowledge is vague and negative – an absence of body rather than the presence of something. But we cannot, and do not, expect to *feel* Spirit. We accept readily that God is invisible and that we cannot see him; we seem reluctant to accept that he is inaudible and that we cannot hear him either. Poetic and ill-advised talk of the 'still, small voice' can mislead us. The 'voice' of God is not 'still' and 'small' because it is a whisper from another plane, although we might like to give it a soft, romantic tone. We may deceive ourselves into thinking that we are being generous by listening for *only* a 'still, small voice': 'Nothing *very* mystical, Lord; just a tiny whisper?'

What we are asking for, of course, is not a still, small voice but the 'earthquake, wind and fire'. Our retreat from the 'noise' of the human is a search for the spectacular. Like Elijah we are dazzled by the pyrotechnics on Mount Carmel when he challenged the priests of Baal to call down fire on the offering of bulls. When they failed, Elijah called down a fire from God which incinerated the offering. When Queen Jezebel sent soldiers after him he prayed to die, but was told instead to go to Mount Horeb and await God's command. Elijah, like ourselves, was depressed at the bleakness he found on Mount Horeb when all that he experienced of God was a 'still, small voice'. The 'still, small voice' is stiller and smaller than we think; but it is certainly in the earthquake, wind, and fire as well as in the minor rumbles of everyday life. The only 'voice' is in the turmoil of life, not in some sequestered refuge. It is the voice of faith; an awareness rather than a feeling of God's presence. It will not make us glow as feeling does – but it will still be there the next morning.

This is not to deny those occasions when a long lovely sensation of recollection may overtake us. Without any day-dreaming we are unaware of the passage of time: the soul speaks to God in a torrent that is as calm as it is full. There seems to be complete harmony, and even symphony, in the orchestration of all the parts of us. This may simply seem to happen and such 'intensive care' will not be given frequently because it is not usually necessary; it is not the way our God-given nature is made to work. God will decide when we need special treatment.

In her short story, 'The Daughters of the Late Colonel', Katherine Mansfield describes two elderly spinsters, cowed by their ogre of a father, who are rendered incapable of thinking for themselves after his death. They consider that the idea of arranging with the undertaker to bury their father in the cold ground without his permission is audacious to the point of rank impertinence. In a delightful scene the vicar, trying to calm these timid souls, hesitantly suggests 'a *little* Communion?' [italics added]. Ladies' size? The two sisters are frightened of their own shadows, never mind an encounter with the Godhead, and recoil in terror from even a 'little Communion'.

The story is a caricature, but it contains a realism in presenting a common situation in which we can shrink from exposure to God, and try to decide how he should, and should not, meet us. But we cannot dictate to him how loudly, how softly, how clearly, how vaguely, he should speak to us. He knows us and what is best for us. He knew the two ladies in Katherine Mansfield's story; he knew their timidity, and he would have spoken to them with that in mind.

His creation of us, of what we consider the ordinary, boring, humanness of us, is more wonderful than any miraculous or mystical experience. He speaks to us through us. We are not merely the recipients of God's speaking: we are the channels through which he is speaking to us, not in a purely instrumental and passive sense, like telephones, but in the way our individual personality filters God's message. Again it is a question of seeing creation as continuous: God did not make us; he does make us. And we change even within ourselves: not only am I different from someone else; I am different from the person that I was yesterday; I am different when in a different mood; I am always changing, while remaining 'me'. I do not of course change into someone else, but I change within. And God notices. My very 'being', as the word indicates, is essentially Present. But if that seems too metaphysical, consider a more obvious example of God's speaking to us through us in the Present.

Take a medieval cathedral. Behold the mass of masonry which was hewed, fashioned, and raised up to God's glory. It is indeed breathtaking, because when we look at such a building we see not only the artefact but the artisans who made it centuries ago. If we do not think of them, if we do not ask 'How?' or even 'Why?' the wonder is lost. So much for the cathedral: now look at the quarry which provided the stone. From that same earth did God hammer and chisel the brain and bone, arms and legs that make up the human being. The same earth is plundered both for cathedral and cathedral-maker. It is not therefore sufficient to wonder at how such a building was created; we must go further back and wonder at how God made the men who made the cathedral. Those hundreds of men swarming like ants over the quarry and the primitive scaffolding are not only men, but God-made men. So the cathedral is not merely echoing the voices of medieval men long dead; it is the voice of God speaking to us through those men as well as through the cathedral they made.

Before man said, 'Let there be a cathedral!' God said, 'Let there be man and woman!' Of course the cathedral does not speak only to us who gaze on it now; it spoke to the very men who made it while they were in the process of making it: 'Who gives you the power, the motive, for raising me to God, but God?' The cathedral, built to God's glory, is not our repayment to God, but yet another gift from God to us. Prayer likewise is speaking back to a God who has already spoken to us, and who is always speaking. We will never succumb fully to the atmosphere of a medieval cathedral, and never see or hear God in it, if we see only the finished cathedral. We have to balance simultaneously in mind and imagination the massive shaped structure, the shapeless unquarried stone and the minuscule men who swarmed all over it. That is the toil and sweat – and possibly blood – which is the wonder. That is where we must see our prayer.

'I don't seem to be getting anywhere in prayer.' There can be a suggestion of a whine about that remark; and would we recognize the 'anywhere' if we did get there? How do we know what 'there' is like? A more appropriate adverb might be 'here'. When we listen to ourselves we are in fact listening to the God who is empowering us both to speak and to listen. That 'ordinariness' is the still, small voice; if we want more we may be seeking the earthquake, wind and fire.

If, however, we insist on God's speaking in concrete, perceptible, black-and-white expression, we have that too – in Scripture. But Scripture comes through the 'body'. The last verse of John's Gospel offers a fascinating insight into the sacramental nature of Scripture:

Now Jesus did many other signs in the presence of the disciples, which are not written in this book; but these are written that you may believe that Jesus is the Christ, the Son of God, and that believing you may have life in his name (Jn. 20:30–31).

This is perhaps the most touching part of John's Gospel. In his account of all that Jesus said and did we see of course the love of Jesus; here we also see the love of John – for us. It is all written 'that you [too] may believe – [as I did]'. Perhaps one proof of the success of Jesus is his influence on John in turning him into an evangelist. Picture John in rather the same way that we see Saint Jerome in El Greco's portrait. He is surrounded by manuscripts, with copies of his own handiwork torn up and re-written, scratching his head for the right word, racking his brains for the exact recall of events he himself witnessed: all so that we too 'may believe, and ... have life in his name.' That is sacrament. Before God gave John the 'Gospel' he gave him 'John', with John's intelligence, literacy, literary style and Johannine insight.

The Gospel according to John is precisely that – written and interpreted, emphasised and meditated upon according to *John*. To John, through John; to us through John. So-called 'problems' regarding discrepancies in the four gospel accounts must be seen as enriching rather than bewildering or annoying. Different sources, cultures, emphases, addressees, circumstances – all reveal Gospel *through* humanity, *through* creation: simply 'through' sacrament. Mark, Matthew, and Luke leave their own genetic fingerprints. The Spirit guides them in the Truth; all other 'guiding' was given in their fathers' loins and their mothers' wombs. And, of course, the Jesus who was 'Gospel', and is 'Gospel', is 'throughness' personified. He is God's speaking enfleshed: we cannot get more 'through' than that. We cannot contemplate anything more sublime, nor anything earthier. John's Gospel which, compared to the other three, is almost ethereal, states with emphasis, not that the Word was made Man, but that 'the Word was made *flesh*'. Exactly the same thing, but an emotional stress on the earthiness, weakness and sacramentality of humanity. So when we hear – and hopefully listen to – 'This is the Gospel of the Lord' and respond, 'Praise to thee, Lord Jesus Christ', we might also breathe a prayer of thanks to those who wrote the Gospels. For because of them and all the other Sacred Writers, we can hardly complain that God is silent; we say, 'This is the Word of the Lord'. And what is said in Scripture is at times only too audible. But it will never deafen us, never frighten us, never overwhelm us, if we realise that it comes not only through the human evangelist, through the human as well as divine Jesus: it comes through us. Not only to us, but through us, in such a way that we can grasp it, apply it, pray it.

There is an old story about a stranger asking a native how to get to a locality, and the native answers: 'Well now, if I was going to that place I wouldn't start from here'. This tends to be the advice we follow in prayer. But in reality we *must* start from 'here', and in a sense stay 'here'. There is certainly no other place to start, and, in a profound sense, no other place to finish. 'The kingdom of God is within you.' That is the 'anywhere' we don't seem to get to.

This is not an exercise in breaking down cherished beliefs, nor a reduction of the supernatural to the natural. Nor is it a denial of those occasions when God in a sense makes contact beyond the senses: when heart speaks to heart; when the Spirit himself intercedes for us with sighs too deep for words. But even wordless and non-sensory communication is natural, one of God's many natural gifts. But these ways of communing are normally exclusively angelic; and God made us 'lower than the angels'. When I stress God's speaking to us through us, I am pointing out how deeply personal prayer is; it not only comes to me *through* me: it comes to *me* through me. At Caesarea Philippi Jesus, after asking the apostles, 'Who do men say that I am?' followed with the question he was dramatically leading up to, and it is addressed to us too: 'Who do *you* say that I am?' (Mk. 8:27,29).

Prayer of Compromise

The disciple who begged Jesus, 'Lord, teach us to pray' (Lk. 11:1) raised some interesting points. First of all, did he say, 'Teach us to *pray*'; or 'Teach *us* to pray, as John [the Baptist] taught *his* disciples'? I believe that the emphasis was on 'teach *us*', and the request has nothing to do with John the Baptist, nor indeed much to do with prayer. The disciples have seen Jesus praying, but they have seen something more − the *effects* of his prayer on him. He has gone into prayer dispirited and tired, and come out of it vibrant. This is what the disciple wants − the effect of prayer, rather than prayer itself. His plea, 'Teach us to pray' is of course a prayer, but it is the motivation which is striking. The one who prays is the best, or worst, advertisement for prayer.

The reader may already have lost interest because of what has been said about Jesus being dispirited, and it is precisely this implied reluctance to believe in the total humanity of Jesus which causes a blockage in prayer and in our whole attitude to life. We find it almost impossible to believe that the *only* difference between the human Jesus and ourselves was the fact that he did not sin: 'For we have not a high priest who is unable to sympathise with our weaknesses, but one who *in every respect* has been tempted as we are, yet without sinning' (Heb. 4:15) [italics added]. This is a text embodying the fundamental truth of Christianity, yet we disembody it by our own qualifications: 'Yes, Jesus was human but ...' there is only one 'but' − sinlessness; and that, far from diminishing the humanity of Jesus, makes him more human.

'Depart from me, for I am a sinful man, O Lord' (Lk. 5:8). 'And I intend to go on being a sinful man, O Lord. Not seri-

11

ously sinful: heaven forbid! But just sinful enough to make life worth living. Moderation in all things; while I do not want the flames of hell to lick my heels, neither do I want the sun of heaven to scorch my scalp.'

Many will dispute this interpretation of Peter's response to the power of Jesus and see his reference to his sinfulness as not only mitigating the 'Depart from me!' (an injunction normally served on Jesus by demoniacs), but actually making it a praiseworthy acknowledgement of unworthiness. Peter was of course unworthy, though he seldom shows awareness of this in the Gospels, and sometimes has to have it pointed out to him. Luke emphasises the double vocative 'Peter, Peter', used as a kind but firm corrective; in the same way we read in Luke's Gospel, 'Martha, Martha,' when she is bouncing crockery off the kitchen walls to draw attention to her work while Mary sits and soaks up the words of Jesus. In Acts we hear 'Saul, Saul' addressed to the irate and self-righteous Pharisee, en route for Damascus with the blood of Stephen still wet on his hands and a few more Christian scalps for his belt.

'Simon, Simon' is spoken to warn Peter that he will deny Jesus (Lk. 22:31–34). This prediction was forced on a reluctant Jesus because of Peter's boast that he would die for him; indeed he does, but only after denying Jesus three times. There is not too much humility in Peter's protestation of sinfulness, if that is what it was. Perhaps instead he has a well-founded suspicion that Jesus is going to make demands on him that would disturb the middle-of-the-road attitude that most of us settle for. 'I don't do anyone any harm' is seen as a modest, almost apologetic, disclaimer; in point of fact, of course, it is a colossal claim to holiness. Not that any of us would want to be accused of sanctity: we might feel obliged to live up to it. That is precisely what Peter is afraid of, and not without good cause. He is aware of a conflict between prayer and compromise. At times the prayer in us is choked by something not at all dissimilar to the guilt of Coleridge's Ancient Mariner, when the old sailor, who has been the unwitting cause of the deaths of the crew, is denied even the power to pray.

> I looked to Heaven and tried to pray;
> But or ever a prayer had gusht,

A wicked whisper came, and made
My heart as dry as dust.
                    The Rime of the Ancient Mariner, IV, 244–7

The Ancient Mariner felt remorse and deep contrition about the
past. When we are faced with prayer the situation can be more
complicated. We are aware of praying one thing, and doing
another – and fully intending to go on doing it. How can we
pray to the 'Holiest in the Height' when we live lives that are
not holy? How can we say all those lovely things we think we
should say to God about giving ourselves radically to him when
we have such unlovely reservations? Not only do we hate the
guts of the person kneeling alongside us, but we intend to go on
hating them. Or it may be a case of divorcees, re-married against
their consciences, who see a blank wall between themselves and
redemption, and disqualify themselves from prayer on the
grounds that a relationship with God must be neat and tidy
according to standards set by ourselves and not by God.

Fortunately relationships with God do not have to be neat and
tidy, and many people in seemingly impossible situations pray
well precisely because they feel forlorn, since all prayer is really
'prayer of compromise'. When we hear statements like 'Prayer is
for everyone', we think that this refers to all those who sincerely
want to be close to God. But prayer *is* for *everyone*, including
those who have not the slightest intention of coming close to
God; which means becoming aware that God is close to us.

Take now a concrete and typical case of compromise such as
that of Peter: the kind of person with average religious commitment. What do we do in a situation where we fear that prayer
cannot be sincere because our behaviour falls short of our ideals
and we intend to keep things that way? The first thing is to pray.
The second is to realise that compromise will never spoil prayer,
but prayer can seriously damage compromise. We can be embar-
rassed by our awareness that we do not really mean what we say
about prayer being a gift of God. Such an awareness can,
however, be a gift of God for others who will benefit from our
discomfort, and it is essential to realise that our prayer always has
a positive effect on other people – whether or not we perceive
this. Prayer, like compromise, is always 'social', always involving
others, or it is not prayer. We can see the link between compro-

mise and our social obligations in the account of the Rich Young Man.

In Matthew's Gospel we are told that a rich young man comes to Jesus, asking what he must do to enter eternal life. The original Greek construction shows the unpleasant selfishness and insensitivity of this man: 'Good master, what *one* thing must I do and, having done, be saved?' In other words, *how* do I get my passport stamped with a visa for heaven? Jesus immediately sees the conflict in the man (and sees it as the conflict of humankind): 'Why do you ask me about what is good? One there is who is good.' (Mt. 19:17)

We cannot palm off our compromises on an indulgent spiritual director; compromise has to intrude into prayer, has to *become* prayer, a naked encounter between me and God. The rich man already knows this, and Jesus is simply telling him that he (Jesus) knows that he knows this. Then Jesus dismissively tells him to keep the commandments. The rich man, rather curiously, asks 'Which ones?' Jesus rattles off those forbidding stealing, killing, adultery, the destroying of a reputation, and ends, significantly, with the commandment which includes all the others: 'You shall love your neighbour as yourself.' The rich man will not be fobbed off with what he mistakenly believes to be a routine formula, and he then comes to the heart of his problem, which he had earlier expressed by the words, *tí eti hustero*; 'What do I still lack? What is it that festers within and gives me no peace?' That is the classic 'prayer of compromise'. The young man tells Jesus that he keeps all the commandments: and that he keeps his wealth. He had not of course kept all the commandments: certainly not in the opinion of Jesus, who sees the poverty of the poor and the reality of this man's wealth as some fracture of *the* commandment, to love.

It is at this point that (in Mark's Gospel) Jesus 'looking upon him loved him' (Mk. 10:21). The 'looking' is a loving gaze into the man's heart, into his conflict; a compassionate gaze into his struggle and compromise; a looking that is healing as well as merely revealing, not a neutral X-ray that dispassionately announces 'malignant' or 'benign' with equal composure. It is an *understanding* look. To return to Matthew: 'If you would be perfect, go, sell what you possess, and give to the poor' (Mt. 19:21). This is where prayer really locks onto reality, and bares from bandages what should be exposed to the scalpel.

It is here we see that the settling of our compromises is not some enclosed cosy little chat between ourselves and God but a strong fresh breeze blowing us out of ourselves, as the mighty hurricane of Pentecost blew the apostles out of the attic, but only after settling intimately and quietly 'on *each* of them' in '*parted* tongues of fire'. The rich man is being told that he will settle his personal problem only by settling the problems of others – in this case the poor. The important word is the '*Go*, sell what you have ...' Not too much soul-searching; leave my surgery, or confessional, and leave yourself alone! Give to the poor! Don't search for peace of mind, you won't find it; give to the poor, and peace will find you. But the treatment is ruthless. Not merely, '*Give* to the poor!', but, '*Sell* what you have!' What he has is not the crude cash of the *nouveau riche*, but the right accent, children in private schools, membership of the right golf club, and so on ... all that painfully acquired status of coming out of the right stud: all to be *sold*; assets to be liquefied; which means that the rich man himself has to liquefy, to melt in love. Later Jesus says that it is easier for a camel to pass through the eye of a needle than for the rich to enter heaven. Liquid can pass through the tiniest eye of the most minute needle, and the young man must become liquid love. His selfish self-scrutiny is breezily blown away (the poor cannot afford the luxury of being spiritual hypochondriacs).

Jesus is saying, for the umpteenth time, that what we regard as private, personal, 'spiritual' problems are also the problems we inflict on others. On a 'Family Fast Day' we fast, not primarily to make ourselves thinner and fitter, but to make the starving fatter and fitter. Our prayer of compromise will reveal to us the sheer brazenness of our complacency, in that we can quietly and philosophically test our spiritual blood pressure when speedy and decisive action is needed for others. '*Others*' is what prayer of compromise is about, and Jesus may have felt like giving the rich young man a kick in the pants, which in his brusqueness he seems to do. That, however, is only one side of the matter.

'If you would be perfect', says Matthew's Jesus, 'sell what you possess and give to the poor.' 'Perfect' is what we all want to be; that is the problem which causes the unease that can make us leave prayer alone. The young man 'went away sad'. The fact that he went away *sad* may mean that, spiritually, he did not go away at all. His 'sadness', his awareness of compromise, brought him to Jesus in the first place; it might have disabled him from ever getting Jesus out of his system. 'If you want to be *perfect* ...' The word translates the Greek *teleios*, related to *telos* – 'far'. The teleology of an acorn is to become an oak tree which, at the acorn stage, is *telos* – far from an oak tree. Perfection is the process of our development, our growth: not unimpeded, but relentless in spite of obstacles. Perfection does not mean an absence of the slightest moral blemish. The rich man is called to perfection; we all are. Jesus does not say, 'If *you* would be perfect'; nor, '*If* you would be perfect', because we all 'would' be perfect, but if we are not prepared to be radical in our Christian commitment the 'would' is mere wishfulness, called by theologians 'velleity'; we insist on perfection, as a caterpillar insists on leaving the mud and cabbages to take wing into the sunlight.

There is of course a difference. Acorn and caterpillar have no choice in moving towards oak and butterfly: we do have a choice. We can stunt ourselves; *we* can compromise. But we have no choice about avoiding the pain caused by such stunting. So when we look God in the eye in prayer we do not *create* a problem; we *bring* a problem – to God, the only one who will 'look upon' us as he looked upon the rich man. He also 'looked upon' the apostles who witnessed the incident and were dumbfounded: 'Who *can* be saved?' they enquired in resignation, or spluttered in despair. No one, replied Jesus, unless he is aided by God. 'With God,' however, 'all things are possible.' So we involve God, by prayer. All things are then 'possible', but not easy.

Our reluctance to pray because of our weakness is a neat attempt at self-deception. Within compromise deception comes at many levels, as in Peter's profession of sinfulness. 'Depart from me, for I am a sinful man, O Lord'. There is a Dickensian character who personifies a slightly more subtle evasion. Mr Skimpole of *Bleak House* is an apparently lovable, improvident character who blandly runs up debts charged to his too–permissive benefactor with disarming remarks that he himself attaches no importance to money, that he is a 'child' in such matters. It is a surprise to no one except his too-indulgent host that he bares his fangs at the end, and is revealed as a calculating parasite. Our apparent 'easy-goingness' is a façade when we compromise. Much easier to see this in others, of course. Push and probe a little into the carefree character who laughingly confesses that he 'completely forgot' a responsibility and you may see the smile freeze to glacial coldness and granite hardness; 'I damn well *will* be carefree' is hissed through gritted teeth. Weakness of course, but not the 'lovable' weakness we, like Peter, tend to plead. To lead this kind of irresponsible, easy-going existence needs steely determination. A soft and receptive heart is found in the perfect.

Our compromises in prayer take a battering because we are forced to think of others; our unease eases them. We find this in most of the prophetic denunciations of hypocrisy in the Old Testament. Isaiah confronts us with precisely what we dread in prayer. 'Bring no more vain offerings ... cease to do evil, learn to do good ... correct oppression; defend the fatherless, plead for the widow' (Is. 1:13,16–17). He disturbs the hierarchy we impose on the gravity of sin. We normally see serious sin in sexual excess, where it certainly lies; but we tend to make the mistake of limiting it to that area. The three sexual sinners described in the Gospels are women; all three are forgiven and treated with gentleness and sensitivity by Jesus. On the other hand, the only two examples of punishment actually described as taking place in the next world concern *social* sinners: 'Dives', the rich man who neglected Lazarus the beggar, (Lk. 16:19–31), and those who did not succour the needy (Mt. 25:41–46). Even though the prostitute in the gospel is referred to as 'a woman who was a *sinner*', (Lk. 7:37), it is not Jesus who sees that as the worst sin. We use the word 'weakness' of male and female sexual sin, but exploitation of the poor and violent crime are greater moral weaknesses. Jesus follows the example of those such as Isaiah who, after fulminating against sin in general, narrows the cause of his contempt to those sins that cry to heaven for justice: 'Seek justice, correct oppression; defend the fatherless, plead for the widow' (Is. 1:17). But our ability to compromise is so resilient! Those widows and orphans are fortunately distanced from us by two and a half millennia, and our own guilt can be comfortably distanced too.

But it will not help us to limit thoughts of injustice to Isaiah two and a half thousand years ago: keep to the place and people you live with! Think of the downright lies we tell or imply by evasion or silence. We are told to pass on an important message; we do not pass it on. We say that 'it slippped my mind', and think that the casualness blurs or even blots out the guilt. It does not; we cannot diminish our guilt. We are, in this case, liars as well as unjust. We use our positions of authority for perks and privileges instead of for service; an injustice. We ignore or 'forget' people, either through crass insensitivity or through a pretence which may be caused by anger and jealousy; injustice again.

Let us suppose that we are dimly aware of this and even bring it into an examination of conscience and to the sacrament of reconciliation; we may hear ourselves saying, 'Now about my prayer life!!!' But the exclamation marks would not be ours, but those of the victims of our pettiness if they could overhear us. They do not need to overhear us; they know of our stupid attempt (hopefully unsuccessful) to separate prayer from behaviour. Those who see us praying and who suffer at our hands must know only too well how successfully we separate our prayer from our behaviour, perhaps because they do the same thing themselves. When we are seen at prayer, others may rightly think, 'He should be talking to me, not to God; I could tell him a thing or two.' Our 'prayer' can put others off prayer.

When in Matthew's account of the Sermon on the Mount Jesus said that we should leave our gift on the altar and be reconciled with our brother first, and then come to offer our gift, he was not referring to any bitterness in ourselves, but to a bitterness we have caused our brother to feel against us, precisely because of our behaviour: 'If you ... remember that your brother has something against you', if you have infected him with your bitterness, go and pray to *him* first. Even if you never come back to offer your gift at the altar, you will have offered a more acceptable gift at the shrine of your brother. To hurt someone and then leave them to stew in resentment while we walk demurely to the altar drives the 'Isaiah' in everyone else to frenzy.

Our double standards, our ability to 'move the goal posts' and our infuriating distinctions between prayer and life, are the very reasons why we need to pray the more, although we frequently see them as reasons for giving up prayer completely. In

Shakespeare's play, Hamlet is driven to the edge of madness, and over the edge of homicide, not only by obsessive vengefulness because of his father's murder and his mother's seduction by the murderer, but because of the hypocrisy and pretence involved. He looks, almost admiringly and unbelievingly, at his murderous uncle Claudius topping up the guests' cocktails, and is utterly bewildered at the over-turning of reality and truth, so that he splutters: 'O ... smiling, damned villain! ... That one may smile, and smile, and be a villain'. (*Hamlet*, 1.4.106–8.) Quite simple, Hamlet, if you put your mind to it. But Hamlet was young, and did not live long enough to learn the art of pretence. As far as the point I want to make is concerned, the heart of the play is the scene in which Hamlet sees his hated uncle praying. He draws his sword, thinking that this is the best time to strike, because Claudius' back is turned. But his uncle's back is not turned to heaven. Hamlet wants to kill him 'that his heels may kick at heaven' in his downward dive hellwards. In fact Claudius is making the classic prayer of compromise; he repents his crimes, but not their fruits. But he *is* in the act of praying about it; and if Hamlet had killed him then, there would indeed have been a serious danger that Claudius would have gone straight to heaven! For Claudius, the killer, has received the *grace* of awareness of compromise; and grace it is: painful, but grace-full.

'Though your sins be like scarlet, they shall be as white as snow' (Is. 1:18). This is a deeply consoling reminder of the infinite mercy of God, and none of us should ever recover from the shock of the sheer power of this divine mercy which sweeps away all our sins. This keenest delight is ours when we feel a heavy burden of guilt lifted from us, when our sins are like scarlet. But what about the times when our sins are a mere pale pastel pink? Do we *want* to be as white as snow? After all, the whiteness of snow will show up the tiniest speck of dirt; and we may want those specks to remain. It is here that we need to reflect on how strong God's mercy really is. We think of divine infinite forgiveness as showing its power most clearly in the forgiveness of the worst sins; but this is not quite true. God's forgiveness of course knows no bounds, and the most heinous offences, if sincerely repented, will most certainly be forgiven. But the power of God's forgiveness is even greater than that. Not only does God forgive the worst sins; he forgives even the least sins! Which means that he can so love us as to make us *want* the 'least sins' to be forgiven, the petty sins that Peter may have felt he had the right to hold on to.

Prayer can change this attitude by loosening our hold on our peccadillos. And this will be done by allowing other people into our prayer; to them our slight imperfections are not slight. Our compromise hurts them. On the other hand, if I practise self-denial, this prevents others being denied; my self-restraint removes restraint from my neighbour. The skirmish with our compromises will be happier and healthier if we allow others to be involved; prayer is *social*. Peter Chrysologus writing in the fifth century voices our fears: 'Prayer, fasting and mercy: these three are a unit ... If a man has only one of them, or if he does not have them all simultaneously, he has nothing' (*Sermon* 43).

Not as discouraging as it sounds. On the contrary, it is most encouraging and consoling – for others. And those 'others' will keep coming into our prayer. But they are not intrusive; and they are certainly not 'distractions'. It is of course these 'others' whom we confront in our prayer of compromise: 'As you did it to one of the least of these my brethren, you did it to me' (Mt. 25:40). That was not only what the damned heard; it was what the Blessed heard. We damn and bless ourselves according to how we wrestle with compromise in regard to others. And, of course, when these 'others' pray, *we* become the 'others'. Every one of the Ten Commandments, including the First, is a commandment to love others as we love ourselves. Every obligation of ours is the *right* of another. Even the idolatry commandment really forbids us to worship the ultimate idol of sin – ourselves. And that particular idol damages its worshippers.

'Come now, let us reason together, says the Lord: though your sins are like scarlet, they shall be as white as snow.'(Is.1:18) Unbelievable! An Old Testament prophet, of all people, seeing God as inviting sinful men to 'reason together' with him about the hypocrisy of the sacrifices offered while they are exploiting the poor, using their God-given authority to pervert justice – in the name of justice. The hypocrites always provoke the fiercest onslaughts of Jesus because they practise a vice that is so *like* virtue, while being its opposite. Yet a certain kind of hypocrite can be sincere in preaching, to himself and others, principles which he constantly reminds his listeners that they should live up to while failing to live up to them himself. To these God says, in a calm after the storm of the diatribe, 'Come, let us reason together.' It is not as astonishing as it seems.

When Jesus says in the Sermon on the Mount that we must love those who hate our guts, he is inviting rather than commanding, coaxing rather than threatening: 'You love loving, don't you? You hate hating, don't you? then why allow anyone to stunt you?' 'Reasoning together' is the way in which prayer compromises and continues to do so for as long as compromise lasts: which is as long as we last.

It is difficult to pray with compromise; it is impossible to pray without it. This is in peaceful contrast to the thunderous invective poured out immediately before when the prophet says 'Ah, sinful nation, a people laden with iniquity' (Is. 1:4). But the violence of the prophetic outbursts are ultimately the rage of human nature at injustice, and at the degradation we detest even as we descend to it. No anger is greater than anger at oneself. To say that such upheavals of fury are human is not to deny the divine; on the contrary, it is to prove that God is *in* the human made by him, in his image and likeness which 'will flame out, like shining from shook foil'.* But the 'reasoning *together*' involves God, and this will calm us, as did the 'Martha, Martha'; 'Saul, Saul'; 'Simon, Simon': the first use of the name spoken loudly to catch the attention; having caught it, a softer voice. The 'reasoning together' cools things down, makes us bring the ruthless glare of mind to play on clouded fear and encrusted protective layers that are in fact fungal or suffocating. Our compromise may seem to have been very carefully thought out, but that is because we have reasoned by ourselves. In prayer, however, we 'reason together'.

The 'reasoning together', the conversation between ourselves and God, though on the face of it daunting if not terrifying, is in fact a great relief. We have come to the end of the road. We now face the truth we earlier fled. And the truth is that 'no one *can* serve two masters' diametrically opposed to one another. It is not a question of not being *allowed*, but of not being *able* (Greek *dunatai*), to serve two such masters. That futile attempt creates a

---

* *The Poems of Gerard Manley Hopkins*, 4th edn., ed. W.H. Gardner and N.H. Mackenzie (Oxford, 1967). p. 66. 'God's Grandeur'.

conflict. Our energies tear us apart by straining in different directions; the very opposite of that integrated force Paul describes with regard to his own struggles in his Letter to the Philippians: 'straining forward to what lies ahead' (3:13). Earlier in the same Letter he describes a conflict – though a delightful one – when he declares himself 'hard pressed between the two' (1:23); meaning that he cannot make up his mind whether he wants to 'depart and be with Christ' through death, or remain alive to preach the gospel. Not at all a bad conflict, but still a conflict. When he 'strains forward' there is a stretching of every sinew, but all in one direction towards a single end.

When we 'reason together' with God in prayer our struggle takes on motivation and direction. There is no more flight, no more hiding, no more squinting as we try to seek our fulfilment in opposing directions. Our 'eye' is then 'sound' (Mt. 6:22), which seems to mean that we have found the right direction; we are no longer blinded to true values; we see clearly. Such illumination is not a blindingly original insight, but an opening of our eyes to what has always been there, to an instinct which will give us no rest until we obey its insatiable demands for radical perfection: the instinct that led the author of the classic prayer of compromise, Augustine of Hippo, to move from 'Make me chaste, but not yet' to the only true conclusion: 'Thou hast made us for thyself, O God; and our hearts are restless till they rest in thee.' The pain of this surrender to God is bearable, if only because the alternative is unbearable. When sinful Simon became post-Pentecostal Peter he too must have made a significant alteration to his first awe-struck statement: '*Stay* with me, for I am a sinful man, O Lord.'

Prayer of Forgiveness

Prayer, as we have seen, confronts us with our own compromises and such a confrontation, far from being a deterrent, should be regarded as the strongest motive for prayer. Of all the compromises we refuse to face, the most tenacious is our unwillingness to forgive. This is partly because such unwillingness is frequently seen to be a strength, rather than the weakness we easily detect in laziness, gluttony, sensuality.

Nothing more effectively cripples our emotional and spiritual growth than the inability or refusal to forgive. I say 'inability or refusal' because we who do not forgive may be roughly divided into those who say, 'I can't forgive' and those who grit their teeth and say, 'I *will not* forgive.' Even for the latter it is basically an 'inability' as much as a 'refusal' to forgive. At the heart of this withering lack of forgivingness is the misconception that forgiveness is weakness. If we persist in seeing forgiveness in this way we shall find it utterly impossible; if we see forgiveness as strength, it will merely remain very difficult.

Forgiveness is power. Throughout the psalms we find that God's omnipotence is shown most powerfully in his forgiveness. 'The Lord,' who 'has established his throne in the heavens and [whose] kingdom rules over all' is one who 'forgives' – almost an anticlimax. 'For as the heavens are high above the earth ... as far as the east is from the west, so far does he remove our sins' (Ps.102(103)). A prayer used in the Divine Office begins: 'Lord, you reveal your mighty power most of all by your forgiveness ....' (Twenty-sixth Sunday of the Year). It is therefore important to be clear about the relative positions of forgiver and forgiven. We tend to think that there is something weak and yielding in forgiveness, whereas it implies inflexible resolution. When someone hurts or humiliates us, we often see ourselves as going down, and the assailant as going up: the perpetrator seems to gain an ascendancy over the victim, as if the victim were '*victus*' – conquered.

In reality the opposite is the case. The offender goes 'down'; the offended goes 'up'. The one who inflicts the injury sinks through sin, and through being the one in need of forgiveness. It makes not the slightest difference whether or not he or she wants forgiveness. The one offended 'rises', not because of being offended against, but because of being in the position to forgive or not. When we forgive we do so not from a footstool but from a throne. The footstool is reserved for the one in need of forgiveness. When we forgive we have not only power, but a kind of divine power, since we are in the position of God, the ultimate Forgiver. The offender has rendered himself powerless by being in *need* of forgiveness.

'Heal my soul, for I have sinned against you' (Ps.40(41):4)). What an outrageous plea this is! What brazen impertinence! Heal *my* soul, for I have sinned against *you*! Imagine our reaction if some fiend who has destroyed much of what made our lives worth living asks us for healing! 'But the psalmist says it to God', we say. It is not good enough to say, 'Oh, it's all right for God to heal those who sinned against him, but impossible for us.' We are in fact asking for the gift of being *able* to forgive, reaching out to the fringes of the deity by asking for what is divine. The command is to forgive seventy times seven times. When Peter put the question to Jesus: 'Lord, how often shall my brother sin against me, and I forgive him? As many as seven times?' (Mt. 18:21) one can almost hear Peter's voice rising in apprehension as he goes as high as 'seven', his tone suggesting that this is six times too often. Jesus' first words reassure him, 'No, not seven times ...' As Peter is sighing his relief there comes 'Seventy times seven!' An indefinite number of times! Always! But it is worse than that. Peter probably thought that it meant only (!) that he had to forgive his 'brother' every offence – which it did. (Heaven knows what he thought about forgiving enemies!) But it also meant forgiving the *same* offence many times; always. Peter's problem was that forgiveness seemed *only* an obligation rather than a grace. 'Forgive and forget!' is a wise suggestion, a wish; it can never be a command. If I have a reasonable memory I shall not forget past offences, and I shall remember those committed against me more clearly than those I have committed against others. But forgiveness does not demand amnesia. One fine day the cruel memory of a past injury re-inflames the wound. And I sigh, or swear, 'Not that again, Lord; I have forgiven that once, and it nearly killed me. Do not make me jump through those hoops again!' But the Lord is telling me that those 'hoops' are the means of my growing in holiness; also that it is possible not only to forgive without forgetting, but also to forget without forgiving. The forgotten but not forgiven may haunt me until I finally forgive.

Our prayer for 'forgiving-ness' is an almost over-reaching ambition; until we realise the nobility of the 'human' made in the image and likeness of God. Shakespeare can help here. In *The Tempest* the exiled duke-magician Prospero has the opportunity to avenge himself on his usurpers. Doing his bidding in this revenge is the elfin spirit Ariel, who finally announces that things have gone far enough, which prompts Prospero to ask incredulously if Ariel is actually capable of feeling compassion; of feeling anything?

ARIEL   ... if you now beheld them [*Prospero's erstwhile*
                              enemies, now victims], your affections
                Would become tender.
PROSPERO   Dost thou think so, spirit?
ARIEL   Mine would, sir, were I human.
PROSPERO   And mine *shall*.
                Hast thou, which art but air, a touch, a feeling
                Of their afflictions, and shall not myself,
                One of their *kind*, that relish all as sharply,
                Passion as they, be *kindlier* mov'd than thou art?
                              The Tempest. 5.1.18–24. [italics added]

Pride and anger make Prospero tender; and the same emotions, paradoxically, can do the same for us. Forgiveness is indeed a sharing in a divine gift, and therefore a strength and power given to human nature; but also, and conversely, it springs from an awareness of human weakness prompted by the same divine grace.

The most persistent and pernicious obstacle to forgiving is, as we have seen, the conviction that to forgive is to be weak, to 'give in'. Two people quarrel, and the quarrel leads to a long silence, perhaps for months or years. If they are thrown close together one hour can seem an excruciating eternity. One of the quarrellers, after long experience, perhaps has the wit to realise that an instant breaking of the silence is imperative. The one who does not, and never can, break the silence may preen himself: 'I did not give in; I have an iron will.' He has proved only that he clings pathetically to the rags and tatters of what he imagines to be dignity by hugging to himself a canker that corrupts. He should be screaming, 'Heal my soul, Lord, for I have sinned against you; and intend to go on sinning against you.'

Shakespeare's Shylock, who has been spat upon by the Venetians, sharpens his knife for the 'pound of flesh' which is his 'due'; and who can blame him? His race, religion and person have been ridiculed, and he now has the perfect opportunity to exact vengeance. And Portia, in her plea for mercy, points out that mercy 'blesses him that gives' as well as 'him that takes'; and that, far from being weakness, forgiveness is 'mightiest in the mighty'. But the real force of her classic speech in *The Merchant of Venice* is that she invokes the very opposite of sentimentality or weakness. She tells Shylock that he must exact vengeance! And that the most cruel vengeance he can wreak on the so-called 'christian' Venetians, is – to forgive! To make them really grovel, to cut them more deeply than his knife, by inflicting upon them – forgiveness. They who preached forgiveness would be forgiven by the Jew who practised it; they would never forgive him for that!

'Whatever you bind on earth shall be bound in heaven, and whatever you loose on earth shall be loosed in heaven' (Mt. 16:19). This clearly refers to the power of the church to forgive sins, a point made more explicit later (Mt. 18:18; Jn. 20:23). The text can also mean, 'If you loose [forgive] on earth, *you* [the one who forgives] are loosed in heaven' – and also on earth. As long as we refuse to forgive our enemies we remain enslaved by them; when we forgive we release ourselves also. We need no gospel to tell us this.

Saint John's emphasis – almost obsession – with Truth and its symbols such as Light, and its personification in Jesus who is Light and Truth, is a reminder that Jesus came to 'restore'; to redeem by revealing Truth. He is a Light that darkness cannot extinguish. His Light, which is himself, casts a glow on loveliness, but also a harsh glare on ugliness; it separates fact from fiction, truth from untruth. And how we need this revelation when trying to forgive! Forgiveness is based on Truth, and one of the most fiendish tortures we can put ourselves through is to imagine that in order to forgive we must believe that there is nothing to forgive. I may think that in order to find peace of mind through forgiving I must say to myself, 'So-and-so did not really intend to hurt me; I am too sensitive.' But on occasion I can be absolutely certain that real hurt was intended; he damned well *did* mean to hurt me! Face that, or no peace of mind is possible.

The ultimate *reality* of forgiveness is the fact that we are considered by God to be worth redeeming. Because of that worth, because we are so loved by God, we notice, particularly in the Old Testament, that there are countless references to God's 'anger'; and yet how pathetically easy it is for Israel to wheedle forgiveness out of God. We see the artfulness of the psalmist as he uses his very weakness as a strength in his utterly confident plea for forgiveness: 'For he [God] knows of what we are made, he remembers we are but dust.' (Ps.102(103):14) And God allows himself to be so cajoled. In the Old Testament we see on the part of God the 'pretence' of *not* forgiving. It convinces no one. We see the same thing in the behaviour of parents towards their erring children, especially their infants and tiny tots. Parental 'anger' is wafer-thin; a child's tear, or a toothless smile, and the 'anger' dissolves into what it always was – love. To forgive is often easier than not to forgive, though this cannot be the case with 'Father, forgive them; for they know not what they do' (Lk. 23:34). If these words seem to glide effortlessly from the lips of Jesus on the cross, they might as well have remained unuttered. They did *not* come easily. He 'in every respect has been tempted as we are, yet without sinning' (Heb. 4:15). But he *was* tempted. In John's Gospel Calvary has a very slight whiff of anaesthesia, as the executioners hold up to Jesus a sponge soaked in vinegar. It was an act of rough compassion, which Jesus did not reject. His words, 'I thirst' almost

certainly referred to his consuming love, which nailed him to
the cross, but he graciously sips the vinegar; and gratefully, since
the loss of blood must have left an agonising thirst; and that sip
could have slightly hastened his death, while dulling the pain.
But the real anaesthetic can perhaps be seen in the text from
Luke: 'Father, forgive them; for they know not what they do.'
Forgiveness *eases* the one who forgives. The less easy the
forgiveness, the greater the ease it brings. And this at the hour of
the Lord's death.

The prayer which gives us both the essence and motive for
forgiveness is the Our Father, which by the all-inclusive 'our', not
'my', points to our blood-bond and sin-bond; and consoles us that
it is a *Father* we ask for forgiveness, more prodigal in love than the
father in the 'Prodigal Son' parable, the father who replies to the
elder brother's contemptuous 'this son of yours' by a firm correc-
tion to 'this your brother'. Yet the Our Father has a somewhat
tortuous syntax: 'Forgive us our trespasses, as we forgive those who
trespass against us'. It seems to have three possible meanings, all of
them blasphemous if they were not ridiculous:

i) 'You see, Father, how we forgive; do thou likewise!'

ii) 'Forgive me to the degree in which I forgive others (and
no more).' – which would leave me doomed and damned.

iii) If I do not forgive others, the Father will not forgive me.
In other words, God will retaliate; he will allow my unforgiv-
ingness to envenom him into the same: 'Two can play at that
game; if you don't forgive others, I will not forgive you.' – blasphemy if it were not absurdity.

Matthew's comment on the phrase is not helpful: 'For if you
do not forgive men their trespasses, neither will your Father
forgive you your trespasses' (Mt. 6:15). But God *will* forgive my
trespasses; he will forgive my unforgiveness. He will not allow
me to block his forgiveness by my pettiness. But there is one sin
that not even God can forgive, and it might be taking an apple
or taking a human life; it is the sin that does not want to be
forgiven. And although my unforgiveness of others is spiritually
forgivable, psychologically it is not; I cannot, with all my
hypocrisy, recoil from forgiving and extend my arms to be
forgiven at the same time. Contortions like that defy the basest
insensitivity. What then do the words mean, 'Forgive us our
trespasses, as we forgive those who trespass against us'? They

mean that instead of making a deal with God – 'You forgive me and I'll forgive him' – we ask for *two* graces: the grace to be forgiven and the grace to be forgiving. We do not need to be told that we need grace – and much grace – to forgive. Yet in another way we ask for only one grace – the grace to make us aware that God has truly forgiven us. It is not a question of not being forgiven because we do not forgive, but that we do not forgive because we do not really feel on the pulses that we are forgiven; we limit God's forgiveness by our own. If I really believe that God forgives me, as a Father, then that forgiveness will overspill onto others. If I am truly aware that I am totally forgiven, I may not need to forgive others; I may not notice that there is anything to forgive.

The Pharisee and the
Tax Collector

'Two men went up into the temple to pray, one a Pharisee and the other a tax collector. The Pharisee stood and prayed thus with himself, "God, I thank thee that I am not like other men, extortioners, unjust, adulterers, or even like this tax collector. I fast twice a week, I give tithes of all that I get." But the tax collector, standing far off, would not even lift up his eyes to heaven, but beat his breast, saying, "God, be merciful to me a sinner!" I tell you, this man went down to his house justified rather than the other ...'

(Lk. 18:10–14)

After The Prodigal Son and The Good Samaritan this is probably the most loved of the parables. It has the usual Lukan 'pairing' method (Good Thief – Bad Thief; Poor man – Rich man; Samaritan – Priest, Levite). It is a parable about conversion, and principally about the role of prayer in conversion: the prayer of petition, and the prayer of repetition. It is specifically about prayer for forgiveness and, apart from the prayer of the Good Thief (to which it bears a striking resemblance) 'Jesus, remember me when you come in your kingly power' (Lk. 23:42), it includes the only explicit prayer for forgiveness in the gospels: 'Lord, have mercy on me a sinner!' Many asked Jesus for mercy, by which they meant clinical healing. This tax collector asks for the healing, the radical healing that goes to the root of the primary tumour, sin, and uproots it. This eradication is, of course, always effected by Jesus when he heals the sick. To believe that Jesus would heal someone without forgiving his sins would be a blasphemous accusation of meanness, if not deception. Jesus did not torment the stricken by granting 'mere' remissions (all those healed are now long dead); he healed the whole person, not merely in the sense of clinical healing, but also of that deep-seated sadness and hopelessness which may still confront us when we bounce back to physical and mental health. 'God, God, forgive us all', says the doctor in Macbeth after witnessing the sleep-walking of the tormented and demented Lady Macbeth. As a doctor he has seen enough human anguish to know that God alone could give the healing that was wholeness. The tax-collector knew it too; he wanted total healing; he went to God for it. And he got it.

'Two men went up into the temple to pray.' The typically Lukan contrast – and this parable is also about how not to pray – '...one a Pharisee and the other a tax collector.' Had Luke said, 'A Pharisee and a tax collector went into the temple to pray', the dramatic climax and contrast would have been lost, and we are meant to be surprised. It is hard for us today to feel the shock to Jesus' audience, but we must enter into their feelings. The Pharisee was an upright citizen; the tax collector a downright rogue. Jesus' audience expected the Pharisee to pray properly; the tax collector – well! Think of a critical situation in your life where you felt yourself to be beyond prayer and redemption, and you begin to get a notion of what is meant here by 'tax collector'. Those who first heard this parable had him doomed and damned immediately, with what might seem to be good reason, as we shall see. The parable is addressed to those 'who ... despised others', by which Luke meant particularly the Pharisees – which includes most of us.

Jesus' audience would have expected the story to develop very differently: the Pharisee's prayer would have been edifying, that of the tax collector something of a joke, and not in the best of taste. Indeed, after hearing the Pharisee's prayer, and before Jesus' comment on it, the audience would have found it quite acceptable, at least in part. 'I thank thee, God ...'. Had he dropped dead there and then, the prayer would have been excellent; but he goes on to ruin it: 'I thank thee, God, that I am not like other men, extortioners, unjust, adulterers, or even [for his eye catches the tax collector, so why go further?] like this tax collector' here. Here! What on earth was a tax collector doing here? For 'here' is the temple, and the tax collector must have seemed like the abomination in the sanctuary.

When we read this parable we think that it is only the prayer of the tax collector which is to be imitated. But that of the Pharisee comes temptingly close to being an excellent prayer. In fact, if Luke had not explained beforehand that the parable was directed towards 'some who trusted in themselves that they were righteous and despised others', we might have been able to rescue the Pharisee's prayer, which is in some ways delightful and thankful. The psalmists frequently thank God for keeping them from the 'ways of sinners'; and they too go into detail about those 'ways'. Psalm 118(119), the longest psalm in the psalter and a rhapsody on God's Law, praises God in ecstatic terms for keeping the psalmist on the right lines, which is exactly how he sees the Law; not dusty volumes and inextricable red tape, but God's loving hand guiding, leading, pointing the way to the hesitant human. But the psalmists thank God because God has rescued them; the Pharisee thanks God because the Pharisee has rescued himself – if he needed rescuing at all.

If we look at the erring ways of others and say, 'There but for the grace of God, go I', we are saying, unlike the Pharisee, 'There but for the grace of God am I actually going now.' The 'grace of God' does not refer to one redemptive moment, to one traumatic conversion; it is continuous. This is why the Pharisee's prayer is potentially so beautiful. 'God, I thank thee.' There is nothing like the prayer of gratitude to galvanise us into deep thankfulness. 'I fast twice a week, I give tithes of all that I get.' This is well beyond the demands of the Law which was satisfied with one tenth of certain crops only. The mandatory fast days for everyone were the Day of Atonement, and four other days in memory of the destruction of the temple. Pharisees however fasted every Monday and Thursday, and on these days some of them would not even drink water. So the Pharisee has something to thank God for, in that he has received the grace to fast. The question is, Does he really thank God? Instead of being a heartfelt sigh of relief and sheer joy at being preserved from sin after being forgiven, the prayer dives into the swamps of selfishness. The Pharisee thanks God that he does not need to thank God for forgiveness or protection: not consciously and cold-bloodedly like that of course; he is not so stupid or insensitive.

The name 'Pharisee' means 'separated one', or 'not like others': different, by being better acquainted with the Law and more observant of it. But when our Pharisee disowns 'others' he is not remotely thinking of tax collectors; they are too bad to be included even among the 'others'. So when he then says he is not 'even like this tax collector', he spits out the 'this' in disbelief at seeing the wretch disfiguring the temple by his presence. If only he had known what the tax collector was seeking! But the Pharisee can dismiss tax collectors from his mind: he himself is not 'saved' from sin; he is inoculated against it, or so he thinks. Yet he still believes that he has prayed. Curiously, when he mentions his almsgiving and fasting – two of the three principal duties of the Jewish people (almsgiving, fasting and prayer), he does not mention the third one, prayer, perhaps because he is 'praying' about the other two. I do not detect any pity in Luke for the Pharisee, but Jesus felt it. Jesus would have spoken in the language people understood, and his description of the Pharisees was a blistering one, but love was there too. For the Pharisee is a pitiful, even a tragic, figure. Throughout his life he has tried his hardest to observe the Law to the letter – which is immeasurably better than ignoring it while mouthing about hypocrites.

The tragedy of the Pharisee, as we have seen, is that he is so near to prayer and yet he wastes his opportunity. He went into the temple, the place of asking, and he did not ask. He left as poor as he had arrived. The tax collector 'went down to his house justified.' The 'going down' to his 'house' suggests all the release and restfulness which comes after an arduous ordeal. God alone knows what efforts he had to make to respond to the prompting of grace to enter the temple and a completely new life: almost like entering a tomb-womb, where he dies and is reborn. He must have been utterly exhausted, not with the words of sorrow that poured from him, but from the sheer nervous stress his decision to repent had caused him. We should not under-estimate this.

The tax collector was a criminal. This fiend was not worthy, on the face of it, to occupy the same house as the Pharisee, still less the same house as God. Yet there he was! Admittedly he stood 'far off', possibly in the outer court; but he was there. He belonged to an unholy fraternity who bid for 'farms' (latifundia) or tax districts from the Romans. The publicanus, to use the Roman designation, used his 'farm' of people by fleecing them to the skin and milking them dry. No salary was attached, but it was not voluntary work either. Provided that the tax collector could supply the Romans with what they considered to be slightly above a fair taxation, he was free to exact more himself, which he cheerfully did. Qualifications for the post were few but important: ruthlessness, lack of patriotism and moral scruple, and, above all, a most detailed knowledge of every hen and even egg on the farm. And heaven help anyone giving incorrect returns!

At Matthew's customs post it was a question of paying duty on goods to-ing and fro-ing between Mesopotamia and the Mediterranean ports. Hard to travel that caravan route without going through Capharnaum, and harder still to go through Capharnaum without going through Matthew; or rather, without Matthew going through you. The penalties for gliding through the 'green tunnel' when you should have gone through 'red' were not pleasant. So tax collectors earned money, but not respect, to put it mildly. They bought their friends of either sex, and flouted the 'Law' which flouted them. They were well and truly 'sinners'. The Romans themselves despised them; admittedly a doubtful insult. More importantly, Jesus himself seemed to share a belief in the equation: 'tax collector equals sinner'. In speaking of the love which even the depraved feel for their friends, Jesus says, 'Do not even the tax collectors do the same?' (Mt. 5:46). But in the parallel passage in Luke we have: 'For even sinners do the same' (Lk. 6:33). Tax collectors have never been popular, but in Roman times it was an 'occupation' rather than a 'profession'; a sub-culture of outcasts, who were nonetheless men with power over the pious and honest. The tax collector in our parable says it all: I am 'a sinner.' We believe him. If he were not a sinner the parable would be pointless.

The Greek indicates that not only does the tax collector do and say things in the temple (beating his breast, keeping his eyes on the ground, confessing his sinfulness), but that he keeps on doing and saying them: the prayer of repetition. This offers an interesting insight into prayer. In Matthew's account of the Sermon on the Mount we are instructed not to heap up empty phrases as the pagans do. Jesus does not say that we should keep our prayer short; when he suffered in Gethsemane he prayed the more, and seemed to think that one hour was the minimum in time of temptation. But what did he say? 'My Father, if it be possible, let this cup pass from me; nevertheless, not as I will, but as thou wilt' (Mt. 26:39). As far as we know, these are the only words he said, repeating them over and over again.

In Matthew's sixth chapter, Jesus gives us the Lord's Prayer immediately after the injunction not to drone on and on. The Our Father is delivered in staccato sentences unlubricated by conjunctions, as if a telegram were being pounded over the wires at great expense; or as if one were breathing one's last, in which case prayer would hardly consist of polite observations about the weather. 'Get to the point!' is the message.

In Luke 11 the content of the Lord's Prayer is very similar. When they ask to be taught to pray, the apostles are given an even shorter form of the prayer rapped out with the same terseness. 'Pray like this!' – 'You don't need to be taught to pray. Pray for the essentials! And then pray it again!' The tax collector needs no such advice. He knows what he wants, what he needs, and he asks for it; many times, in the same words. Repetition in such situations is good for the soul. It only bores others – never the one who repeats. And in prayer we are the ones who do the talking. If we are drowning we might bore others to death by shouting the same word 'Help!' But we ourselves shall probably not be at all bored by such repetitious screaming. Until someone hooks us on board a boat, 'Help!' normally suffices. We see no reason to change the word. In a happier context, lovers slip into what seems to the detached observer a boring and repetitive 'I love you.' They never tire of saying it or hearing it. They insist on it, in fact. Repetition again!

The tax collector, therefore, is a simple soul, as well as a devious devil. He brings into the temple all the beady-eyed greed, cunning and rapacity which made him choose his calling, survive it and rise in it. He has always gone for gold, for the very best; he has not changed. Nor should the grovelling posture of this Uriah Heep mislead us: his eyes stare at the ground; his heart is fixed on heaven. And what does he have the brazenness to ask for? Wealth? No. Health? Not at all. He asks for nothing less than supreme fulfilment, unalloyed bliss, endless ecstasy, deepest tranquillity; his grasping fingers reach out for the most elusive of all blessings – peace of soul; the blessing. Forgiveness. And he gets it! If only the Pharisee had known that! If only we knew it! Do we believe it?

'Lord, have mercy on me the sinner.' The usual interpretation of the parable is that the tax collector saw himself as the greatest of all sinners, the sinner par excellence. That is probably true, but there is another point of view. The Pharisee had caught sight of the tax collector; could the tax collector perhaps have seen the Pharisee? True, he kept his eyes on the ground, but might he not have lapsed momentarily into one of his shifty glances upwards? The tax collector could be saying: 'Lord, the Pharisee is holy; have mercy on me who am not.' Or, 'Lord, you see before you two men; give your mercy more to the one who needs it more – me.' It would complete the irony if the tax collector's response to the Pharisee's contempt was respect. If only either of them had known the Pharisee's need for mercy! 'Seek first [God's] kingdom and his righteousness', says Jesus (Mt. 6:33). The tax collector has the effrontery to do precisely this. He does not ask for a king's ransom, or an earthly kingdom: he seeks the kingdom of God. And he then discovers to his unutterable joy that 'The kingdom of God is within you' (Lk. 17:21). In a desperate but far from despairing situation the tax collector's cunning has been turned onto God. He sees himself as spiritually inferior to the Pharisee. Does that deter him? make him envious? Not at all. His weakness becomes his strength. He asks for the righteousness he thinks the Pharisee already has. He does something even more daring, yet so simple: he takes things literally. He has heard that forgiveness is for all. Instead of keeping that firmly imprisoned in the pages of the Bible, as any respectable person would do, he takes it to include him. His prayer is for everything.

He adopts the humble stance of face to the floor, breast-beating, and the repetitive plea for mercy. Why? Because he brings his life into his prayer. A tax collector would often have wretched tax-evaders on their knees before him, beating their breasts, whining for mercy. This grovelling was the only method he knew for those in dire distress, and his erstwhile victims had been in that situation. Now he saw himself in a similar plight. So he used his sinful past to advantage, hoping that he would be more successful than many of his delinquents. Now he is before the Great Auditor: and 'auditor' is not too fanciful a word here, with its two meanings of 'listener' as well as 'one who deals with accounts'. For the tax collector pleads: 'God, be propitiated [no longer angry] with me ...' The Greek hilasthēti is a plea that he be not punished; not the same as being forgiven, but he is only at the beginning of prayer, and still sees God as a celestial tax collector. Countless repetitions will correct that. At the moment he is at least asking.

He did not 'dare' raise his eyes to heaven; the sword might have been poised over his bowed neck. But he was ready for what God decided. Soon the repetition would change that too, and the eyes would follow the gaze of the heart towards heaven and towards a God who was no longer a hatchet-faced judge. Only repetition dissolved those granite images of an implacable deity. But of course the repetition was purely vocal. The lover's 'I love you', the drowning man's 'Help!', are repetition only verbally; every time the words are uttered they carry deeper emotional intensity, deeper feeling and urgency. The speaker is not hearing his words; the feelings pour out ahead of them, all over them; but the sameness of the words helps by excluding the distraction of groping for new ones. A repeated ejaculatory prayer, if urgent, is not boring. The words do not change, but the speaker is transformed.

The preceding parable of The Widow and the Unjust Judge (Lk. 18:1–8) has a profound bearing upon this one. There is the usual Lukan contrast: a widow, then a symbol of defencelessness and neediness (see Luke's Widow of Nain) on the one hand; and an unjust judge on the other. No one was more powerful under God than a judge with power over life and death. This very power, if abused, made the judge a distortion of nature, a hideous freak. Unjust judges brought out the most blood-curdling curses in the imprecatory psalms. But this widow is persistent. The one thing she has is an unconquerable determination to get justice by hook or by crook, and the only power she can muster is that of making a nuisance of herself: so much so that the judge, 'who fears neither God nor man', fears a 'helpless' widow who, precisely because of her weakness and lack of ability to manufacture an ingenious ruse, will give him no rest from her pestering which drives him to administer unaccustomed justice.

The widow's ploy is persistence, which is also repetition. She speaks a language the unjust judge understands only too well. The tax collector speaks a language he himself understands. He has seen his victims grovel, and it has impressed him: so he grovels too. He has seen them cringe and whine for mercy: he does the same.

When the tax collector Matthew rejoices in the call of Jesus he celebrates in the only way he knows; not by shouting Alleluia, not by going on a quiet Retreat, but by throwing a party to which he invites not only Jesus and the other apostles, but also his former colleagues and their girl friends. The Pharisees ask indignantly: 'Why do you eat and drink with tax collectors and sinners?' (Lk. 5:30). A good question: where did the money come from to pay for those cocktails? But many of Matthew's former victims, like those of Zacchaeus, would quite possibly have received 'rebates' to correct 'clerical errors in assessment' and so on. Matthew's party was his prayer of joy and thanksgiving. Conversion means change, but change within the same person; not turning one person into another. The person we were before conversion is of infinite value before conversion – or we would not be worth converting. It is we, not another, who must turn. It was when the Prodigal Son saw his sinfulness, we are told, that 'he came to himself' (Lk. 15:17). Matthew was more like the real Matthew at his party than he had ever been before. When we come to God we bring our true selves, otherwise we are not making our prayer: it is not us praying.

'Lord, have mercy on me, the sinner.' It is difficult to exaggerate the importance of the repetition. After all, there is nothing else the tax collector wants to say, so why bother? He is already asking for absolutely everything; what can he possibly add? As a hard-headed negotiator he finds that the words he uses perfectly express what he wants to say; so why change them? Change takes time, and he does not have time. He has wasted too much of his life already. Why not simply repeat to God the words from the heart? And not so much to God, who reads his heart without words, but to himself. For the words of prayer are for us who pray, not to enlighten a God who knows them already. But while the tax collector is saying the same words over and over again he is listening more and more intently to himself saying them. And after about five hundred repetitions, he realises that God is talking back. How?

The images swimming before his eyes are those of his victims, tortured, bankrupted, driven to crime or vice, their houses repossessed. Phantasms of a fiendish reality perpetrated by him, they begin to choke him with grief, and the same words probably flow faster. Perhaps he misses out a word, or says the same thing twice in one sentence. Sometimes the urgency is close to panic. He has offended God because he has hurt his fellow human beings, but now the ill-gotten money has been returned: amends must already have been made, insofar as he can manage – or he would not have been in the temple at all. But full restitution is impossible, so how much more impossible to appease God? He repeats the words over and over again, and the image of an Auditor God fades and dissolves before his misted yet spiritually clear eyes into the face of a loving Redeemer.

As the repetition continues, the words are perhaps interspersed with silence – a silence that is listening to the echo of each word, relishing the idea behind the word as it slips off his tongue, for the very repetition has served to make word and idea merge. Eventually the tax collector may not be able to hear his own words because of the ideas and feelings, but the words are still needed: they are never intrusive. At that time it was the custom for Jews to pray aloud, and, as we saw earlier, repetition never bores the speaker. But now there is a change in the prayer: 'Lord, thank you for having mercy, and continuing to have mercy, on me, the sinner.'

As we said, the prayer of the tax collector has to be understood in the light of the preceding parable about the Widow and the Unjust Judge. We might be inclined to bracket the four characters in these two parables by placing 'widow – tax collector' on one side of the comparison, and 'Unjust Judge – Pharisee' on the other. And that is correct, but surprising. For the tax collector before his conversion is much closer to the Unjust Judge than is the Pharisee, who is as law-abiding as the widow. But in the case of the widow it is justice which is gained through prayer; in the case of the tax collector it is mercy. And yet it is the Unjust Judge who is made to take the place of God. For Jesus is saying, 'If an unjust judge will hearken to persistence, how much more will God?' Just as he said, 'If you then, who are evil, know how to give good gifts to your children, how much more will your Father who is in heaven?' (Mt. 7:11)

Nevertheless the tax collector, before his prayer, is like that Unjust Judge, and we must not accept too casually the spectacle of his grovelling for forgiveness. This man had been in power, and could have remained there. Spiritually he seems the underdog compared to the Pharisee; socially he is certainly the outcast, 'separated' in a way very different from 'Pharisee' – the officially 'Separated One'. And yet in terms of real power the Pharisee is still the underdog and vulnerable to the exactions of the tax collector. The latter's implied protestations of powerlessness are so pervasive that we may lose sight of the effort it must have cost him; for his conversion and its implications in terms of his livelihood would still be there the next morning. In the temple we hear what he said to God; before that, God had had something to say to him. Before the tax collector did, he was done to. All prayer starts from this. Yet in one way the tax collector has not changed his spots. A new kind of rapacity is there. For before leaving the temple he loots, plunders, pillages it: not of its precious vessels, but of something infinitely precious. He walks out of the temple, out of the house of God – with God.

Prayer of the Prodigal

'There was a man who had two sons. The younger one said to his father, "Father, let me have the share of the estate that will come to me." So the father divided the property between them. A few days later, the younger son got together everything he had and left for a distant country where he squandered his money on a life of debauchery.

'When he had spent it all, that country experienced a severe famine, and now he began to feel the pinch; so he hired himself out to one of the local inhabitants who put him on his farm to feed the pigs. And he would willingly have filled himself with the husks the pigs were eating but no one would let him have them. Then he came to his senses and said, "How many of my father's hired men have all the food they want and more, and here am I dying of hunger! I will leave this place and go to my father and say: Father, I have sinned against heaven and against you; I no longer deserve to be called your son; treat me as one of your hired men." So he left the place and went back to his father.

'While he was still a long way off, his father saw him and was moved with pity. He ran to the boy, clasped him in his arms and kissed him. Then his son said, "Father, I have sinned against heaven and against you. I no longer deserve to be called your son." But the father said to his servants, "Quick! Bring out the best robe and put it on him; put a ring on his finger and sandals on his feet. Bring the calf we have been fattening, and kill it; we will celebrate by having a feast, because this son of mine was dead and has come back to life; he was lost and is found." And they began to celebrate.

'Now the elder son was out in the fields, and on his way back, as he drew near the house, he could hear music and dancing. Calling one of the servants he asked what it was all about. The servant told him. "Your brother has come, and your father has killed the calf we had been fattening because he has got him back safe and sound." He was angry then and refused to go in, and his father came out and began to urge him to come in; but he retorted to his father, "All these years I have slaved for you and never once disobeyed any orders of yours, yet you never offered me so much as a kid for me to celebrate with my friends. But, for this son of yours, when he comes back after swallowing up your property – he and his loose women – you kill the calf we had been fattening."

'The father said, "My son, you are with me always and all I have is yours.
But it was only right we should celebrate and rejoice, because your brother
here was dead and has come to life; he was lost and is found." '

(Luke 15:11–32)

We love to identify ourselves with gospel sinners provided that
they are appealing and eventually repent. But in the 'beautiful
story' of the Prodigal Son we also need to see the 'hard centre'
of Luke who, alone of the evangelists, stresses the need for
dogged perseverance when he says that to be a disciple of Jesus
we must take up our cross 'every day' (9:23). Luke, like
Matthew and Mark, records the heart of Christ's mission: 'I
have not come to call the righteous but sinners to repentance'
(Lk. 5:32; see also Mt. 9:13, Mk. 2:17). This of course refers
to the fact that before the coming of Christ some sinners
thought of themselves as 'righteous', while others knew
perfectly well that they were sinners, and these were the ones
who listened to the call – the 'righteous' believed that they had
already heard it.

We are all prodigals, although our stories may be less
dramatic. The man who is bored at 'having nothing to confess'
in the Sacrament of Reconciliation fails to realise that he too is a
prodigal. We can never understand our forgiveness until we
understand our sinfulness, any more than we can appreciate food
or warmth without the experience of hunger and cold. 'I came
to call sinners' means 'I came to *call* them sinners so that I could
call them from *being* sinners.' The first grace is to be made aware
of one's own sinfulness.

By itself, the prayer of the Prodigal does not teach us this –
we need to hear his father's reaction as well, and we also need to
dismiss the idea that the Prodigal Son was necessarily a high-
spirited youth with his heart in the right place, wherever his
brain might have been. He may not have been young at all. We
only know him to be 'younger' – than his brother. In fact the
Prodigal's behaviour may indicate that he was *not* so young; and
that was the problem. He is saying to his father, 'If you think
that I am going to wait for you to die while I slave away the best
years of what's left of my life, forget it!' Not a lovable black
sheep, he wants to get his hands on the cash before he is too old
to enjoy it in the only way he understands enjoyment.

In Luke's Gospel the Greek word *azōtōs* indicates a life of total depravity which includes sexual over-indulgence. The elder brother's snarling and contemptuous remark hurled at their father underlines it. 'This son of yours has devoured your living with harlots.' The Prodigal has spent not only his money, but himself – just as he wanted. His binge is his fulfilment. When his last penny and his last 'friend' have gone he can sigh 'It is consummated!' The spendthrift is really the meanest of misers: he does not give, he buys; women, drink, escape – they are all for himself.

'I will go to my father!' says the Prodigal, when everything else has gone. This is decisive. Psalm 31(32) offers the somewhat similar example of a man enmeshed in an inextricable tangle of sin who suddenly makes an equally radical decision. The psalm opens with a beatitude: 'Happy the man whose offence is forgiven ... to whom the Lord imputes no guilt!' This is the happiness that comes not only from forgiveness, but from forgiveness where none had previously seemed to be possible. 'I hid my sin and my spirit wasted away,' he recalls. Then, faced with the utterly hopeless task of disentangling his sins strand by strand, he suddenly decides: 'And then I said, "I will confess my sins to the Lord"'. He hurls the lot at God with, 'You sort it out!' And, inevitably, 'You, O Lord, forgave me.' This is perhaps what Peter had in mind when he said, 'Cast all your anxieties on [the Lord]' (1 Pet. 5:7).

When the psalmist says, 'I hid my sin' he knew that he was covering with a bandage what should have been exposed to the scalpel. His confession is a release. But the decisive word is 'I *said*'. That is speaking; that is prayer; that is escape: and escape *is* prayer. This is what is at the heart of the Prodigal's explicit prayer. And yet the prayer had actually begun at his father's house because his father has returned to *him* – not of course that he had ever left his son. The Prodigal says to himself, 'How many of my father's hired servants have bread enough and to spare?' He *remembers* the paternal home, the 'hacienda' on which all have enough to eat. But it is not simply a pleasant scene of well-fed and warmly-housed servants that comes to his mind: it is his father's love; otherwise he would never have plucked up the courage to return.

'When he [the Prodigal] came to himself he said, "... I will arise and go to my father".' But his father has come first. That father – the heavenly father – whom the Prodigal had banished by going away 'into a far country', has leapt across and landed in the pigsty precisely through the Prodigal's remembrance of his love. The Prodigal's prayer, and all prayer, starts with the Father. The love of the father reaches into the sty, hurls the bucket at the whiskered snouts and points the Prodigal homewards – while allowing the son to think he has done it all by himself.

The son's 'rehearsal' is unique in the gospels: 'I will say to him, "Father, I have sinned against heaven and before you; I am no longer worthy to be called your son; treat me as one of your hired servants".' This rehearsal, far from making the prayer insincere, shows the trembling emotion behind it. Faced with an important interview, perhaps the Sacrament of Reconciliation, we rehearse in order to get things right and so as not to waste a golden opportunity. For the Prodigal, the rehearsal is a continuation of his resolve; he needs it in order to steel him to persevere and go home to his father; his prayer is sheer utterance, unburdening.

When the father *sees* the son, and before he *hears* the prayer of the son, he runs out to clasp and kiss him. But his embrace does not stifle the prayer. The timing is exact. The son frees himself from his father's grasp and opens his mouth to utter the words he has been muttering endlessly to himself on the journey home. His father allows him do so and does not interrupt with 'Never mind all that! You're home!' He is allowed to utter every word of confession without interruption. His father only stops him with his own instructions to the servants when the Prodigal is preparing to say 'Treat me as one of your hired servants'; but that is a request, not part of the confession, and is already included in 'Father ... I am no longer worthy to be called your son.' The father *allows* the son to say 'I have sinned against heaven and before you.' He *allows*, but he does not make his son grovel: 'Come on; say it; I didn't quite catch that; speak up; crawl!' The father's greatest gift to his son lies in allowing him to unburden himself. Only then does he send for sandals, ring and robe, and give instructions about the 'fatted calf'. 'Bring *quickly* the best robe ...' Having got that terrible burden off his chest, the son sees the feast as anti-climax; without the *gift* of confession the robe would have been a shroud for him, the banquet a wake.

We are told that the father sees the son 'while he was yet at a distance'. He had been straining his old eyes to see him for a very long time. He runs out to embrace his son because he has *seen* the pray-er, and therefore the prayer. His son's arrival *is* his prayer. Prayer is not our *words* to God; it is '*us* to God'. We do not need to write to someone if we are physically present to them. 'Sorry!' can be said quickly to someone we have accidentally brushed against in a crowd; the same word can be uttered to one we have hated and avoided for years. The word depends on the *situation* for its value. Prayer is *us*; and prayer and 'prayer life' are identical. When the poor Prodigal is muttering his lines to himself his father is listening to every word; he *sees* the rehearsal in his son's face, sees it in his son's presence. God speaks to us most clearly and lovingly in allowing us to speak our guilt to him; by allowing us to escape from ourselves. The father showed his love and forgiveness by *not* interrupting the son: ring, robe, sandals, calf can come later.

'Father, I am no longer worthy to be called your son …' and yet the prodigal has implicitly called himself 'son' by addressing the old man as 'Father'. The father smiles at the contradiction because it comes from an instinct deep within his son, who could never have uttered anything at all had he not regarded him as a father rather than a hard-fisted employer. But the relationship with his father is precisely what causes the guilt of the son, which is the more severe because the Prodigal is aware of the love he has rejected and failed to return. He can only be aware of sin because he is aware of a relationship which has been broken. No matter how harshly he judges himself, he cannot force himself to believe that his father will be harsh. Yet at some level the Prodigal *wants* harshness. He is like Clym Yeobright in Thomas Hardy's *The Return of the Native*. Yeobright experiences terrible guilt at his failure to be reconciled with his mother before her sudden death: where others refuse to believe in God because they are 'punished' too heavily, Yeobright seems to take the opposite view: 'If there is any justice in God let Him kill me now. He has nearly blinded me, but that is not enough. If He would only strike me with more pain I would believe in Him for ever'.*

---

* Thomas Hardy, *The Return of the Native*, Bk.v.ch.1.

The Prodigal sees himself as wicked, which he is; he measures his father's forgiveness in terms of what he himself might be prepared to give under similar circumstances, so he does not ask for *enough*. Unlike the tax collector in Luke's parable of the Pharisee and the tax collector, he does not seek the kingdom. By asking to be taken on as a hired servant he is settling for physical well-being only. Yet when his father runs out to him, the Prodigal can only dissolve into contrition. *That* is the 'kingdom'. Had the father given him the pittance of a place as one of the 'hired servants' which was all that the son was prepared to request, the Prodigal would soon have found that life in the ranch-house with the other servants was far from easy. After one good meal and a night's sleep, he would have awakened to harsh reality, not ameliorated by being under the whip of the Elder Brother. Yet in his willingness to be a hired servant – which his father does not allow him to voice – there is an awareness of his own emptiness. He has reached the state of the repentant Cain: 'My punishment is greater than I can bear' (Gen. 4:13).

The decision of the Prodigal to return to his father 'when he came to himself' indicates that the 'self' he had indulged, away from his father, was not his real self. To drift from God is to depart from the self; a kind of insanity. But the expression suggests that the initiative in the decision to 'return' came from the Prodigal. It did not. As we have seen, it is the remembrance of his father's love which ignites the decision. His father *speaks* to him first; 'no one can say, "Jesus is Lord" except by the Holy Spirit'(I Cor. 12:3).

Prayer of Cain

The man had intercourse with his wife Eve, and she conceived and gave birth
to Cain. 'I have acquired a man with the help of Yahweh,' she said. She gave
birth to a second child, Abel, the brother of Cain. Now Abel became a shep-
herd and kept flocks, while Cain tilled the soil. Time passed and Cain brought
some of the produce of the soil as an offering for Yahweh, while Abel for his
part brought the first-born of his flock and some of their fat as well. Yahweh
looked with favour on Abel and his offering. But he did not look with favour
on Cain and his offering, and Cain was very angry and downcast. Yahweh
asked Cain, 'Why are you angry and downcast? If you are doing right, surely
you ought to hold your head high! But if you are not doing right, Sin is
crouching at the door hungry to get you. You can still master him.' Cain said
to his brother Abel. 'Let us go out'; and while they were in the open country,
Cain set on his brother Abel and killed him.

Yahweh asked Cain. 'Where is your brother Abel?' 'I do not know,' he
replied. 'Am I my brother's guardian?' 'What have you done?' Yahweh asked.
'Listen! Your brother's blood is crying out to me from the ground. Now be
cursed and banned from the ground that has opened its mouth to receive your
brother's blood at your hands. When you till the ground it will no longer yield
up its strength to you. A restless wanderer you will be on earth.' Cain then said
to Yahweh. 'My punishment is greater than I can bear. Look, today you drive
me from the surface of the earth. I must hide from you, and be a restless
wanderer on earth. Why, whoever comes across me will kill me!' 'Very well,
then,' Yahweh replied, 'whoever kills Cain will suffer a sevenfold vengeance.'
So Yahweh put a mark on Cain, so that no one coming across him would kill
him. Cain left Yahweh's presence and settled in the land of Nod, east of Eden.
(Gen. 4:1–16)

Cain became murderous long before killing Abel: one does not
normally become homicidal overnight. He was murderous in
anger and jealousy when offering his sacrifice; and therefore God
rejected it. We must, however, qualify this. Cain's offering was

49

not rejected because of his anger. Rage, envy and bitterness are not at all a bad way to begin prayer; but they are a bad way to end it. The prayers of the psalmists were full of anger; but they poured out this anger *to* God, or aimed it *at* him. They turned their anger into prayer and thus purged it, raising to God the angry minds and hearts they had at the moment of prayer. Cain did not. He hid his real feelings behind the sheaves he shoved in the face of God. So God gave him a great gift; he refused his sacrifice. He did not throw it back at him in cold contempt; he gave him a short, sharp shock, and said: 'Cain, let's start again. Let's have the truth. Tell me what this is all about. Why are you so angry, and why has your countenance fallen? And don't say that it's because I rejected that sacrifice of sheaves; we both know that it goes back a long way before that.' In other words, God is asking Cain to *pray*, or to grope towards prayer through what he was already doing in his sacrifice. The fact that Cain was saying anything at all shows us that he was at the first stage of prayer, even though unable to 'confide' in God. Many a prayer has begun like Cain's and ended like Abel's. It is generally thought that Abel represented the herdsmen, the Jews being herdsmen at the time the text was written down, and the Canaanites – like Cain – were farmers. The story is therefore biased in favour of Abel.

Cain's 'prayer' is the set of exchanges between himself and God; 'conversation' would suggest an ease and friendliness which, though very noticeable on the part of God, is entirely absent from Cain. But there is dialogue of a sort, and the story of Cain enables us to see what prayer should be by first showing us what it should *not* be. Cain's prayer offers a fascinating, if disturbing, example of how in prayer we can come to the 'guts' of our deep-seated problems and their solutions. We seldom know the solutions, so we bury the problems. But the solutions are as real as the problems, and prayer will unearth them. In Cain's prayer God brings the solution to light through the divine device of the 'question'.

It is the method he used when dealing with Cain's parents, Adam and Eve. After their sin they hid themselves in the foliage, as Cain hid his real, angry self behind his sheaves. God called out to Adam and Eve in an apparently innocent enquiry: 'Where are you?' The first reaction of the first sinners was therefore to hide;

and that was their second sin. When they took the apple they doubted the power of God; when they hid, they doubted his forgiveness, the proof of his power. God's questions become more probing: 'Who told you that you were naked?' *Sin* told them. ('O what a tangled web we weave, When first we practise to deceive.') The 'hiding' has begun. As if fig leaves, or trees, or forests, could hide them from God! But one single leaf could hide God from them. If we put our minds to it we can crouch or cower behind even less. Prayer means coming out into the open with arms raised in surrender to God. His questions to Cain, both before and after the murder, are not put to him in order to torment or terrorise, but to persuade and coax him to 'come clean'. Had Cain responded to God before the murder, that murder would never have taken place. God employs questions because Cain has not only to give answers, but also to *hear* himself giving them. And the questions God asks are really being asked by Cain himself: 'Why am I angry?' It is at this crossroads that 'prayer' can become *real* prayer, or remain just 'prayer'. For we can hide behind 'prayers' as well as behind any other foliage.

'My punishment is greater than I can bear.' Cain makes this anguished cry after the murder of Abel has been discovered and punished by God, and he has been sentenced to become a wanderer over an earth which will yield him nothing. But long before this Cain had felt his punishment to be unbearable. His sacrifice had been rejected because God wanted Cain to offer himself instead of his sheaves. But Cain cannot face this in spite of the gentle and coaxing questions: 'Why are you angry? Why are you downcast?' Cain is being asked to admit that his jealousy, anger and self-disgust are his unbearable and self-inflicted punishment, and until he acknowledges this he will never be able to find healing. Until he *says* it he does not really *know* it. Only when Cain is forced to sob, 'My punishment is greater than I can bear', does he tremble on the edge of self-knowledge. He still does not recognise his own arrogance and total lack of self-esteem, but at least, and at last, he openly admits his weakness, indeed his helplessness. God's punishment simply confirmed the state of things that had always existed for Cain.

Let us look at God's sentencing to see how accurately it mirrors Cain's existing situation. 'When you till the ground, it shall no longer yield to you its strength; you shall be a fugitive and a wanderer on the earth.' But Cain had always been at odds with the earth, with everything outside him. He would have torn the stalks from the ground, raping rather than reaping. And as for being a fugitive, he had been fleeing from himself long before his sacrifice was rejected. This has been his problem – hiding behind his sheaves, behind anything. Because of the dislocation in his relationship with the earth there has always been a terrible disharmony between Cain and anything non-Cain, and between the two sides of his personality. He is destructive. He destroys Abel because he is destroyed within himself. He has spilt the blood of his brother, which falls back into the lap of earth, his 'grandmother,' making the womb into a tomb. God dramatically re-creates the dislocation caused by the murder which was in turn caused by the dislocation of Cain. 'What have you *done*?' Earlier God had warned Cain of the dangers of his state of mind: 'Sin is couching at the door; its desire is for you, but you must master it' (Gen. 4:7). Now things have gone beyond thought to action; 'What have you *done*?' Instead of the boil bursting in prayer it has erupted into murder. Then the eerie lowering of God's voice: 'Hush, I can hear your brother's blood crying from the earth. Can you hear it?' But the terrified Cain can hear only his own heart-beat and the throbbing of his blood. And now all reality seems to drift away from him. 'The ground ... shall no longer yield to you its strength.' On an earth bursting with fruitfulness Cain, with every step, treads on desert. Wherever Cain's shadow falls, that part of earth recoils. He touches a flower, and it withers. The contrast between the fragrant, fertile earth and the blighted Cain is absolute. He is like Coleridge's Ancient Mariner who, in a world of salt water, has to scream, 'Water, water everywhere, Nor any drop to drink'. The final isolation is complete. Now, at last, comes his 'true' prayer: 'My punishment is greater than I can bear.'

The power of prayer can be seen in the violence of Cain which prayer alone could control. Cain's sacrifice was rejected because he *hid* himself by refusing to offer his pain to God. True prayer would have been for Cain to offer *Cain*. The sacrifice offered by Abel is not very helpful to us because we know so little about him; he does not live long enough. Yet Christian tradition, from as early as the Letter to the Hebrews, has seen

Abel's sacrifice as a perfect offering (Heb. 11:4). But elsewhere in the New Testament (Heb. 12:24; Mt. 23:35; Lk. 11:51) 'Abel's sacrifice' means the sacrifice that *was* Abel, rather than the sacrifice made *by* Abel. When he offered the firstling of his flock he offered himself; his love, worship and faith. Cain did not offer himself; he held back. So all the force of feeling that should have gone into offering and sacrificing himself exploded into his sacrificing of Abel. Like his parents, he was ashamed to be naked before God, but he could not quench the force within him.

He needed to pray like the 'sinful woman' who gate-crashed the party of Simon the Pharisee, the prostitute who burst into Simon's sophisticated salon, smashed a jar of precious ointment – the wages of her sin – and poured this wealth all over Jesus: her ill-spent life poured out with her ill-gotten gains. The Pharisees were outraged. This 'creature', who had plied her trade by baring her body, now bared her *soul* – even more scandalously shameless! She had committed the sin fatal to a prostitute's profession; she loved. She took a terrible risk as she opened her soul to Jesus, quivering at the enormity, not of her sins, but of the exposure of her deepest 'self' – for the first time in her life. She need not have worried: 'Your sins are forgiven.' (Lk. 7:48) Cain could not achieve this until the very end, when layer after layer had been peeled from him to reveal his shivering soul: 'My punishment is greater than I can bear.' And now the healing.

'Men will kill me!' Cain screams. 'Not so!' God thunders: and puts his 'mark' on Cain. Now no one will dare to kill Cain. Not from fear of Cain, whose 'machismo' is mercifully in tatters; but for fear of God, who protects Cain and has always watched over him. Only now does Cain accept with the deepest relief what he would never have admitted or even known before – his total dependence on God. Cain, and later Esau, felt themselves cheated because their younger brothers, Abel and Jacob, seemed to be preferred. The elder brother, Esau, felt that he had the *right* to inherit; and we tend to agree. We see the choice by God of the younger brother Jacob as 'gift' in contrast to the 'right' of Esau. But Esau was also 'gifted' because he was the first-born; he did nothing to 'deserve' being conceived and born before Jacob.

Cain is now *open* to the truth. 'My punishment is greater than I can bear' comes close to the heart of Cain's real prayer. But it is incomplete until he makes a prayer that seems to come from the damned in hell. 'From thy face I shall be hidden.' Cain, who has lived in hiding from God, now fears that God will hide from him. His anguish is the terror of separation from God. He himself had up to this moment done all the separating; now all defences and pretences are down. But there is still punishment, alongside forgiveness – which is better than no punishment and *un*forgiveness. Cain has God's 'mark' upon him, which means that *others* will see through this. Cain will not see God, but now he knows that God will always see him. Cain's very horror at the thought of separation from God should be carefully examined. He does not fear that God will be hidden from him, but that he will be hidden from God: 'From thy face I shall be hidden.' No: he was never hidden even when he wanted to be.

And God's most enlightening revelation to Cain is the revelation of Cain's own dignity and value. For Cain thought himself worthless; that was the root of his pain, his anger, his jealousy. It is painful when others write us off; it is a disaster when we write ourselves off. 'Why are you angry, and why has your countenance fallen? If you do well, will you not be accepted?' (Gen. 4:6) That is far from rejection but is the reason our faces fall when Jesus tells us to love our enemies: 'If you love [only] those who love you, what reward have you?' (Mt. 5:46) Are you happy in limiting your love like that? You love loving? You hate hating? Prayer is all about answering, as well as asking.

Prayer of Faith

When he went into Capernaum a centurion came up and pleaded with him. 'Sir,' he said, 'my servant is lying at home paralysed and in great pain.' Jesus said to him, 'I will come myself and cure him.' The centurion replied, 'Sir, I am not worthy to have you under my roof; just give the word and my servant will be cured. For I am under authority myself and have soldiers under me; and I say to one man, "Go," and he goes; to another, "Come here," and he comes; to my servant, "Do this," and he does it.' When Jesus heard this he was astonished and said to those following him, 'In truth I tell you, in no one in Israel have I found faith as great as this. And I tell you that many will come from east and west and sit down with Abraham and Isaac and Jacob at the feast in the kingdom of Heaven; but the children of the kingdom will be thrown out into the darkness outside, where there will be weeping and grinding of teeth.' And to the centurion Jesus said, 'Go back, then; let this be done for you, as your faith demands.' And the servant was cured at that moment.

(Matt. 8:5–13)

For a Roman officer to intercede for a slave at all is almost a miracle in itself. Centurions in the New Testament are usually good men, but none like this one, who comes himself instead of sending a messenger to Jesus. It is important to keep this in mind since the same centurion is to utter the words which ask Jesus *not* to come, not to trouble himself with a 'house call'; yet the centurion came to Jesus *himself* and thought it no trouble to do so, although he was a man who had the authority to say to others 'Go!'.

Note his words; he does not simply say that his servant is ill; he gives details: 'My servant is lying paralysed at home, in terrible distress.' That is not a clinical description but the expression of someone who is emotionally involved, who is himself in great distress at seeing the other in pain: and Jesus does not merely listen on occasions like this; he looks: and he reads the worry on the man's face, and sees the love that causes it. So he gathers himself for the journey, almost like a doctor glancing at his watch, throwing a few things into his bag, with 'Well, let's have a look at him' – a natural response since the centurion has stressed that the servant is at home and paralysed and therefore cannot come to Jesus. 'At home' does not mean the bunkhouse; it means at the centurion's family home, so it is clear that we are not dealing with a possessive slave-owner who would speedily disown and evict a useless paralysed slave. And yet the passage is not about love. Rather, we have one of the most moving examples of faith in the New Testament. The centurion responds to Jesus' offer to 'come and heal' by asking for the 'healing' without the 'coming'. And this is the heart of the prayer, rather than his protestation 'Sir, I am unworthy ...'

The centurion tells Jesus 'I am a man under authority myself with soldiers under me; and I say to one, "Go!" and he goes ... and to my slave, "Do this!" and he does it.' Jesus is not merely impressed; he is astonished: 'Truly, I say to you, not even in Israel have I found such *faith*.' Note the emphasis: 'Truly, I say to you ...' And there is stress on the man's pagan background. It is not a question of the centurion being considerate, not wanting to disturb Jesus by asking for a 'house call'; it is the man's *faith* which tells him that this is unnecessary. No wonder that Jesus 'marvelled'.

As a Roman officer the centurion gets results by one word of command, 'Go!' No questions, no explanations, no physical force needed: just the *word*. As a slave-owner the same thing; 'Do this!' and it is done. The word alone is sufficient. So if he, a low-ranking Roman officer, can get results by the word alone, Jesus could do a great deal more! The centurion would have given anything to have Jesus come to his house. He would dearly have loved his reassuring physical presence bending over the sick bed, feeling a pulse or a fevered forehead, giving a blessing; all of which Jesus did many times when he healed. But the centurion grits his teeth and says 'No! Just say the word!' – healing at a distance.

By a strange coincidence the only other case of healing at a distance also involves a pagan – the Syro-Phoenician woman whose demonically-possessed daughter is also 'at home'. She too shows faith, similar to that of the pagan centurion, and is praised for it: 'Truly, I say to you, not even in Israel have I found such faith' (Mk. 8:10; Lk. 7:9). It is as if pagans were so used to being 'far off' (Eph. 2:13) that they were more capable of the 'prayer of distance' than the Jews. 'Say but the word and I shall be healed': the last words we hear at the Eucharist before receiving the Body of Christ. What a challenging paradox! At the moment of Communion, the closest of all unions with God this side of the grave, we hear words of distance; 'Say but the word!' And now the words 'I am not worthy' take on a different meaning. Not worthy of what? Not worthy of demanding an emotional, reassuring, awareness of Christ's Presence. For after Communion the chances are that we will not feel one bit better than before. And we must disown all claims to such feeling. Say only the 'word': 'The body of Christ!' If we demand more we are demanding a 'house call', that Christ should come 'under my roof' in such a way that I 'know' him to be there. He does not need to.

'Who shall separate us from the love of Christ?' (Rom. 8:35.) Paul lists a number of formidable possible obstacles, none of which can effect such a separation. The only thing that can come between myself and Christ is *me*. And often, like Cain, I can even push 'prayers' between me and God; I can separate myself from prayer by 'prayers', or by forcing my feelings between myself and Christ. We cannot demand emotional returns on what we consider to be our religious investment. God is often nearest when he seems farthest, most attentive when he seems aloof.

> On the way to Jerusalem he was passing along between Samaria and Galilee. And as he entered a village, he was met by ten lepers, who stood at a distance and lifted up their voices and said, 'Jesus, Master, have mercy on us.' When he saw them he said, 'Go and show yourselves to the priests.' And as they went they were cleansed.
>
> (Lk. 17: 11–14)

These lepers 'lifted up their voices' because they 'stood at a distance' – because they were lepers. In one of his earliest miracles Jesus had healed a leper by touching him on the head; it was very probably the first time that the man had been knowingly and lovingly touched by a non-leper, and through that touch, as through a poultice, the venom of bitterness was sucked away. All the anger and grief and terror of those years were drawn out. The leprosy was also cured, of course, but perhaps the leper hardly noticed that. Because of the deeper healing he knew that he need never again feel socially, psychologically, and spiritually, outcast. The clinical healing may even have been an anti-climax, an external sign of the more radical healing: of his *roots*.

It was not so with the ten lepers. No hand is laid upon their scabrous scalps. Nor are they told to draw near. On the contrary, they are told to increase the distance: 'Go to the priests!' 'Go!' That word would have been the only greeting they ever received from anybody. 'Go to the priests!' was not in itself a dismissal. The priests could give a certificate of health to a former leper if the leprosy were healed, but priests could not heal; so the lepers were being asked somewhat curtly by Jesus to make an act of faith: 'Go to the priests and by the time you arrive there you will have been healed.'

But the leper referred to earlier was healed *before* being told to go to the priests; our ten lepers have to risk the shame of showing their leprous and unhealed faces to the outraged clergy. They realised that with every step they took they were further from Jesus and nearer to the priests. Was Jesus really sending them away, or was he following behind? Jesus does not impose faith as a price of healing; he gives faith as well as healing and it is the greater gift of the two. The lepers are told to 'Go!', not in in order to humour Jesus, or that they may 'sit up and beg' for their healing, but to engage in the ordeal of faith so that they may be healed from far more than leprosy. They are being coaxed into asking for faith; for everything. And this, in fact, is what they *had* asked for without knowing it when they said: 'Jesus, Master, have mercy on us!' That is the heart-cry of humanity, the unuttered prayer of each one of us. And it asks for everything.

The lepers have made the perfect prayer of petition without knowing it. Their words do not ask for a cure from leprosy. That may be what they want, but it is not what they are requesting. Their cry is for *mercy*. Before the lepers can articulate what they *want*, a cry escapes begging for what they *need*, and in their hearts what they would love to have, but think too much to ask. They knew that Jesus, although some distance away, realised that they were lepers; which is why they were keeping their distance. They knew, or thought they knew, that Jesus would assume that the 'mercy' they asked for was a medical cure. But the cry from their lips came from the *roots* of their misery, bypassing reflection: 'Jesus, cure our sadness!' Not the leprosy which causes sadness. No, the cry was greedier; cure the sadness itself! 'Lord, leapfrog over what we consider the *means* to happiness, and give us *happiness!*' Had they been given another second to be more specific they might have changed their cry to, 'Heal our leprosy!' But the instinctive cry for 'mercy' said everything. They were like babies in their pleading. When a baby cries it does not know *what* it wants; only that it *wants*. It does not need to know more. It cries, and leaves the parents to decode the message. When, by trial and error, the parents get it right, the baby will tell them so – by silence. The lepers, long before they were lepers, knew that they *wanted*; Jesus was attempting to reveal to them *what* they wanted. Their cry said it for them, and to them. The lesson from instinct now had to be driven home.

'And as they *went* they were *cleansed*. The 'went' and the 'cleansed' defy each other; the lepers do not really 'go' at all. The healing means that Jesus had 'gone' with them. His physical absence was the test of their faith in his 'real' presence. It is the situation of the centurion who trusted in the healing of his servant, and needed Jesus 'only to say the word'; the ten lepers, unlike the centurion, do not themselves choose this test of faith; it is offered to them, but not forced upon them. And here is another lesson concerning the social nature of prayer, in that it directly affects other people. The centurion had long since learned this, or he would never have interceded for his servant in the first place.

Jesus was with the ten lepers *before* their healing, precisely because of their illness. He was with them because they were with each other, and they would not have been together if they had not been lepers. Nine were Jews, and the other a Samaritan. We are told that they met Jesus 'between Samaria and Galilee' – border country.

When frontiers are blurred, people frequently know more than a smattering of the language and customs of their foreign neighbours, but this would not have been the case here. An

implacable hatred had existed between Jew and Samaritan for
five centuries, since the Assyrians had transplanted pagans into
the former northern kingdom of Israel and created a hybrid
nation that was neither Jew nor Gentile. But adversity makes
strange bedfellows, and the lepers were all outcasts, united in
being disunited from their non-leprous countrymen. Illness
made the stranger a non-stranger.

The ten lepers were 'experiencing' Jesus through each other
even before he met them. And he told them to go *together*.
When they were healed of leprosy, each would see the faces of
the other nine healed before he knew of his own healing;
perhaps each one thought for a fraction of a second that he was
the only one unhealed; until the others told him. And yet the
only one to return is the Samaritan: not merely to give thanks,
but to know whom to thank: '... praising God with a loud voice
... he fell on his knees at Jesus' feet, giving him thanks.' The
Samaritan thanked Jesus the Jew! And in a loud voice, and on his
knees – no creeping up unobtrusively while the other Samaritans
aren't looking. It is not only a clinical leprosy that has left him.
He had been brought to his knees long before he met Jesus, but
that was the servile abasement to which suffering reduced him;
now he falls down in love and gratitude. For him there will
never again be Jew or Greek or Samaritan – only human beings.

'Where are the [other] nine?' We only know that they were
not where they should have been – on their knees before Jesus.
Perhaps *they* might have returned if the Samaritan had not done
so. Possibly prejudice kept them away; they could not 'pray'
because that Samaritan whom they may have thought of as
having no right to pray was daring to do so. What is certain is
that they had learned nothing.

Prayer of Desolation

'And at the ninth hour Jesus cried out in a loud voice, "My God, my God, why have you deserted me"'(Mk. 15:34; Ps. 21(22)). This psalm, possibly the most harrowing of all the psalms of anguish, plumbs the depths of desolation. It is a psalm of terrible torment, and the opening words come to the lips of Jesus on the cross.

> 'My God, my God, why hast thou forsaken me?
> Why art thou so far from helping me?...
> O my God, I cry by day, but thou dost not answer;
> And by night, but find no rest ....
> I am poured out like water,
> And all my bones are out of joint;
> My heart is like wax,
> It is melted within my breast ...'

(Psalm 21(22))

That first line is the great cry of desolation. It is howled out of an inner emptiness into a world of emptinesses. Total isolation, utter loneliness; and nothing is more terrifying. Naked, separated from friends, soon to be separated from his life; and now from his Father, whom he addresses as 'My God'. Earlier, in that frightful bloody sweat in the garden, Jesus cried to his Father, 'Abba'. But now it is 'My God', as if he were being distanced by this formal address, as if contrasting his shredded humanity with the divinity of God. The words come from Psalm 21(22) in which the psalmist says 'My God, my God'; but that is no reason in itself why Jesus should use them. In Luke's Gospel Jesus, on the cross, utters words from Psalm 30(31), but 'Into your hands ... O *Lord*' is changed into '*Father*, into your hands'. There is no such change in the cry of desolation from Psalm 21(22) 'My God, my God'. The 'Father' is very much God, and Jesus very much man. And a very lonely man. Loneliness in its direst form is the most frightening experience of all for humanity. All fear is reducible to loneliness, including the fear of death. This has nothing to do with a comfortable solitude, a reflective mood, or the holy feeling one may enjoy during a retreat which has been freely chosen and will end when we wish; nor with eccentric self-isolation, or crankish misanthropy. No, utter loneliness leads to panic, the nearest one can get to insanity without actually becoming insane.

The separation and 'aloneness' would have been terror enough had it been inevitable, but Jesus had been pitchforked into this terrible isolation because his 'friends' had chosen to separate themselves from him.

Jesus expected this desertion by the apostles; foretold it, and forgave it before it happened. But it still hurt. Their desertion was bad enough, but now, 'My God, my God, why have *you* forsaken me?' That is very different. Any separation through desertion is a refinement of the pain of loneliness, just as separation through betrayal or divorce can be less endurable than separation through death. Loneliness is in the mind, not in external causes. It is not mere 'aloneness', but an aloneness which can be terrifying as one is thrown in upon one's isolated self. All pain isolates us by making us dwindle to the locus of agony, to the point of the pain. 'A bandage hides the place where each is living', says Auden of the patients in 'Surgical Ward'.* The loneliness of dying is the ultimate separation, as part of the self is taken from another part of that same self. Absolute loneliness, deepest depression, is in the cry of desolation on the cross. But it is also a *prayer* of desolation, and it is prayer in a most astonishing way, because the desolation of Jesus is our consolation: because his mental anguish consoles us as he voices our own torment.

A further source of consolation for us is that Jesus, at his most helpless, is spiritually helped by the prayer and the experience of a sinful psalmist dead for seven centuries. The Saviour of the

---

* *W.H. Auden: A Selection by the Author* (Penguin, published by the Modern Library as *Selected Poetry of W.H. Auden*, 1958). This poem appears in *W.H. Auden: Collected Poems* ed. E. Mendelson, Faber & Faber, 1976, 1991 under the title 'Sonnets from China XIV'.

world is 'saved' in his agony by one whom he came to save. He is not ministered to by angels, not comforted by the 'holy women' who shared his agony from a distance, not by his sinless mother: but by a Hebrew poet who in his own mental agony left a testimony which became known as Psalm 21(22), one of the most anguished of all the psalms, the record of a torment similar to that endured by Jesus. The psalmist, however, survived to tell the tale, or the psalm; Jesus did not. The psalm has a happy ending: the psalmist knew the happy ending when he *wrote* the beginning, but he did not know the happy ending when he *felt* the beginning. And what a harrowing beginning and middle there is in this psalm, as the psalmist experiences the sheer panic and disbelief that comes from whirling in a vacuum where all length, breadth, height and depth are lost; where there is that terrible *emptying*:

> Like water I am poured out,
> Disjointed are all my bones.
> My heart has become like wax,
> It is melted within my breast.

This liquefaction terrifies the sufferer as he feels all that is warm and comforting ooze out of him; all those lovely feelings which give him his identity seep from him; his very self is deserting him. And during all this he can only look on helplessly. This is not a case of being alienated from others, from God; it is alienation from oneself, a state of forlornness bordering on madness (psychiatrists used to be called 'alienists'). There seems to be no room for further agony, but there is; and it has a cruel twist. While all that the psalmist wants to keep within him is haemorrhaging from him, that which he wants to escape from him is fast locked up inside. He cannot even find the relief that comes from *uttering*: 'Parched as burnt clay is my throat, my tongue cleaves to my jaws.' But he does utter, if only to say that he cannot utter, and we have seen how central this is to prayer. But this utterance is now on the lips of the crucified and dying Jesus. The long-dead, sinful psalmist comes to the aid of the Saviour by allowing him the release and relief of utterance, of expression. The psalmist *after* his redemption from agony gives to the Redeemer solace *in* his agony. And whence did the psalmist find those words coming to him? From the Father, through the fore-seen redemption of humanity by the screaming man on the cross. And the Father, whose absence Jesus loudly lamented, was close to him in the words of a sinful, suffering psalmist who himself had felt so distanced from God. The sinner's words were redemptive to Jesus!

The Our Father was the prayer Jesus gave to mankind; Psalm 21(22) was the prayer mankind gave to Jesus. And it would seem to be the most heartfelt prayer ever made by the seemingly God-forsaken Jesus.

But the psalmist had consoled and helped Jesus long before the crucifixion. For this text to come to the lips of Jesus at his dying meant that it had come to his heart and helped him throughout his life. It was a part of him, not a disembodied 'text' from a remote 'Scripture'; and certainly not 'quoted'; you do not 'quote' when hanging on to the shreds of sanity. Yet our deepest feelings often find best expression in the words of others which we have made our own. For lovers, a popular tune can become 'our tune'. For Jesus, Scripture was heard as well as read, felt as well as thought. This psalm said all that he wanted to say, although it was hardly a question of mentally leafing through an anthology – the psalm appeared in his mind and on his lips simultaneously. It uttered itself; Jesus simply listened. He knew the whole of the psalm, and it said *all* that he felt; the ecstasy at the end, as well as the agony at the beginning. But what possible ecstasy could there have been in that cry of desolation? None at all, in the usual sense of the word. And yet it was precisely the ecstasy which intensified the agony; and vice versa.

Jesus felt the keenest desolation, not from his crucifying agony, fiendish though this was, but from the sense of dereliction. He felt forsaken by his Father whom he addressed as 'God'. What sort of feeling in the deserted can cause such pain? Only the deepest love. Jesus was closest to his Father when he felt most alienated from him. Those most in love feel most keenly any separation from the loved one. The pain can be even greater if the distancing is caused by betrayal on the part of the beloved. Jesus does not feel betrayed by God, but he is bewildered at God's 'absence'. There are no stage direction in the Gospels, no tones of voice apart from the occasional 'in a loud voice'; we have to surmise the stress in the cry of desolation. Was it, 'Why have *you* (in contrast to the apostles) deserted me?' Or was it that Jesus, knowing his Father's love, was the more bewildered precisely because of this: '*Why*? I know you love me, so *why* this absence?' Dearly as he loved them, is it likely that Jesus would have had this feeling when the apostles fled?

As we have seen, their desertion did not surprise him; but he would not have been able to foretell the desolation he was to feel when he uttered the cry from the cross. Such desolation is not a proof of love; it *is* love. It is the summit of all those cries from the psalmists: 'My eyes are wasted away from looking for my God.' And, of course, Psalm 21(22), 'My God, my God, *why* have you forsaken me?' The 'Why?' of Jesus echoes the bewilderment and incomprehension of humanity at any suffering. In an almost sadistic way – and I stress 'almost' – Jesus is being humilated into an almost grovelling profession of love. It began in Gethsemane where he cried 'Abba', a more childlike address than the adult and dignified 'Ab' (Father). On Calvary 'Jesus cried out with a loud voice'. The Greek verb used, *eboēsen*, describes the bellowing of a bull! Not only were the words themselves disedifying, but also the way in which they were uttered. 'And when the centurion, who stood facing him, saw that he *thus* breathed his last, he said, 'Truly this man was the Son of God.' When what hung on the cross was scarcely human, never mind divine, the centurion hears coming from his own lips that supreme profession of faith. The scene is dense in paradox. When Jesus the man seems furthest from 'my God, my God' the centurion sees him not only as close to God but identified *with* God, as 'the Son of God'. And Jesus who *feels* 'far off' brings close the centurion who *was* 'far off'. In the light of this, Paul's proffered comfort to the formerly pagan Ephesians takes on an authentic ring: 'But now in Christ Jesus you who once were far off have been brought near in the blood of Christ' (Eph. 2:13). And 'blood' means blood sweated as well as blood shed.

That frightful bellow of desolation with its ugliness is all the more redeeming of all that *is* ugly. It is an exorcism, a vocal titanic battle. It is the opposite of fatalistic hopelessness; a shout of defiance against a now conquered evil. It comes from the pain of love which, anguishing because of feeling distanced, abolishes that distance. When we cease to lament the distance from a loved one, then is the distance increased. When we feel content without the loved one, loneliness becomes solitude. If this cry of desolation is to be a prayer for us, as it was for Jesus, we have to try to '*feel*' what we accept at a notional level: Jesus was *truly* human.

Personal Prayer

Long before the apostles knew that Jesus was truly God the Son, they knew him as a man; a very special man, but a man. It was his humanity, in all senses of that word, which drew them to him, and kept them with him; and, when they left him, brought them back again. Had Jesus not captured them by his human love, human personality, and human speech and actions, they would not have stayed with him long enough to know more about him. His divinity came to them through his loving humanity, or it would never have come to them at all. They had to love the man they saw before they could love the God they did not see. Our prayers must be addressed to this Jesus, this person, not to a divine Unknown, or they will disappear into a void.

When we say that all prayer must be 'through Christ our Lord' it does not mean that we cannot address the Father directly; we do this of course in the Our Father. But who gave us that prayer? It is called the Lord's Prayer, because it was Jesus the Lord who taught us to call God 'Father'. Without Jesus, the Father might have seemed an implacable and remote deity. The very existence of Jesus, before he opened his mouth, never mind preached, revealed the love of the Father and revealed God as Father: 'God so loved the world that he gave his only Son' (Jn. 3:16). When we therefore speak of going to the Father 'through Christ' we do not mean 'through him' as a train has to go through Clapham Junction to get to Waterloo. We mean that in prayer we need to know to whom we are speaking. If I do not pray *to* a person I shall not pray *as* a person. Prayer is not usually emotionally reassuring, but if we disembody it from the 'person' of Christ it has no direction at all – like an unaddressed letter tossed hopefully, or hopelessly, into a post box.

We must have a destination in prayer, for where our prayer goes we go, and hope to go forever when we die. Prayer is communication with what lies beyond death; we must discover a person waiting for us, a living hand stretched out to us, otherwise we are utterly forlorn and fearful. We must learn that it is not *what* is beyond death but *who* is beyond it, the One who has been through death. Not Lazarus, not the son of the widow of Nain, not the daughter of Jairus; they came *out of* death, on this side of death, to the same old life that was to be taken from them again. Jesus alone came *through* death, out the other side, as he tells us through the apostles in that lovely long last discourse which takes up five chapters of John's Gospel (Jn. 13–17).

The apostles are in an 'Upper Room', the room set out for guests in the 'Bed and Breakfast' accommodation which the natives of Jerusalem provided for pilgrims there for the feast. But Passover was, and is, a family feast, like our Christmas. The 'Lower Room' was for the family, warm, intimate. The 'Upper Room' was the setting for a mournful stag-party of northerners dumped in the southern metropolis.

Later, at the Ascension, when the apostles stood and stared at Jesus disappearing into the clouds, two angels, like celestial policemen, addressed them, 'Men of Galilee, why do you stand looking into heaven?' Why men of *Galilee*? As if Galilee were as far from the Jerusalem suburb of Bethany where they stood, as earth was from the heaven to which Jesus had ascended. To the apostles it was. Lured from their Galilean homes by Jesus, they were now in strange and hostile territory. Not only were they forlorn; they were forlorn *Galileans*. But by then they had come to see their destination as Jesus, not a place. But it had not been like that at the Last Supper.

Jesus had spoken of 'going away', and it was clear that it was not the 'going away' of catching the 4.32 from Euston; it sounded ominously like the kind of 'going away' you do not come back from: like death. And he adds, 'You know the way where I am going.' Thomas interrupts anxiously; 'Lord, we do *not* know where you are going; how *can* we know the way?' Thomas does not exactly ask for a map to heaven, but he does

ask for *something*. A mistake. He should have asked for *someone*.
'How can we know the way?' Jesus gazes at him; 'Thomas,
you are gazing at the way'. He says: '*I* am the way, and the
truth, and the life; no one comes to the Father, but by me.'
Thomas has scarcely resumed his seat when up jumps Philip;
'Lord, show us the Father, and we shall be satisfied.' *We*! 'You
can go on your own (painful) way, but leave a map behind
you!' Once again we are invited, challenged, to renew our faith.
Not in the divinity of Jesus – it was the apostles who needed
that; but in the *humanity* of Jesus – the apostles were only too
aware of his humanity! Jesus must have been deeply hurt by
Philip's selfish and insensitive remark: Out of the way, Lord,
and point us to the Father, to our endless, ecstatic bliss, which
you said was with the Father. The reply of Jesus needs to be
seen as that of a human soul that is wounded: 'Philip, have I
been with you so long, and yet you do not know me? He who
has seen me *has* seen the Father; how can you say "Show us
the Father."' Note the wounded repetition of Philip's
wounding question. 'How can you say "Show us the Father?"'
and the use of Philip's name makes the situation more personal,
and respectful.

At the betrayal by Judas, the betrayed Lord does not seem to
say contemptuously, 'Do *you* betray the Son of Man with a *kiss*?'
but to whisper gently, '*Judas*, do you *betray* the Son of Man with
a kiss?' 'Kiss, according to the plan; but change that kiss now
into one of loving remorse! Too late for me, but not for you.
Only you and I will know that the kiss is repentance, not
betrayal.' But there is again the use of the name – Judas –
contrasted with the apparently impersonal reference Jesus makes
to himself. He does not say, 'Do you betray *me*?', but, 'Do you
betray the *Son of Man*?' – your Messiah, your fulfilment, your
heaven. In other words, 'Do you, Judas my friend, betray *yourself*
with a kiss?' Jesus sinks his own personality, but only in order to
save that of Judas. He does the same to Philip in his poignantly
and embarrassingly humble response to him 'Believe me for the
sake of [my] works.' Don't believe because you value me, but
because of my work for you. Don't trust my word, but judge by
the empirically verifiable. Coals of fire on our heads! This self-
effacement, this apparent emptying of his own personality, to
enhance the personality of his mulish and insensitive listeners!

Do we appreciate how hurtful this exchange must have been for Jesus? Only if we believe that he was really human: which we probably do not.

Only if we pray to the person of Jesus *the man*, can our own highly subjective sensitivity become objective, enabling us to change from Thomas and Philip into Jesus. 'Have I been with you so long?' 'Yes, too long! Long enough to see the dust and sweat on you; smell the fear in you!'

There is a reminder here that really *personal* prayer must not be confused with *private* prayer, if by 'private' we mean a cosy and exclusive chat between me and God. That cannot be prayer, only a 'Lord, Lord', while doing our own selfish thing. The 'personal' must include others. Paul had this point made to him somewhat violently en route for Damascus. Unsaddled by the Divine Highwayman, whom he thought safely tucked away in a tomb, he was invited to answer the question: 'Saul, Saul, why do you persecute *me* [not my disciples]?' It is not a question of loving and respecting others because Christ is in them, but rather that Christ is in them *because* they are lovable. We are not 'precious' because we are bought at the price of Christ's precious blood (1 Pet. 1:19); we are bought at the price of his blood *because* we are precious. The value exists *before* purchase, not *after*. It is *we*, as individuals made in God's image, who are most valuable, most precious. We are bad enough to need redemption, but good enough to be redeemable. Only the direct appeal to Jesus in prayer will reassure us about that. In this dependence on the *person* of Christ we face our nervousness and helplessness, and resolve it.

To give an example: about eight thousand miles from home I had to make an enforced and unscheduled change to another aircraft in order to travel another few thousand miles. Decanted with me were a young couple, also from England, with a son and daughter, both under five. The adults were grappling with passports and air tickets, trying to make sense of the metallic noises from crackling loud-speakers: what was not inaudible was unintelligible. The parents were trying to move luggage towards departure gates with their feet, yet the two children were completely calm. Each had one hand in the hand of a parent. One child also had a death-grip on the throat of a battered teddy bear; the other was clutching a rapidly diminishing ice-cream.

Teddy bear and ice-cream were their only concerns. Eight thousand miles from England, they were 'home' because they were
clutching the hands of their parents. If they had been in a shop
very close to home, but found their hands disengaged from a
parental hand, they would have screamed in terror, utterly
disorientated. No use asking them, '*Where* do you live?' The
question is '*Who* do you live with?' Home for them is persons,
parents, not place.

When the disciples return from their first and last 'mission'
during the earthly life of Jesus, they seem to have been
welcomed back by Jesus with a cry of joy: 'I bless you, Father,
Lord of heaven and earth, for ... revealing [these things] to *little
children.*' The 'little children' translates '*nēpiois*', those who are
childlike – not childish – in acknowledging their total dependence on the Father through Jesus. The disciples claimed that
they had done marvellous things 'in your name', so even in their
physical separation from Jesus they acted totally under his influence. In the Acts of the Apostles the confidence of the
missionaries is rooted in the 'name' of Jesus. At this name, Paul
tells us, every knee shall bow.

As children, we accepted our parent's life-preserving instructions about traffic, or the bottles on the bathroom shelf, without
reflecting on whether or not we found them to be wise. Had we
not instinctively accepted parental guidance we should not have
survived for very long. We do not believe in Jesus *because* we
think his words are true; we take his words as true *because* Jesus
said them. Paul preached Christ, not Christianity; we pray
Christ, not Christian doctrine. When the apostles (in Jn. 6) were
asked if they too would 'go away' because of their disbelief in his
Eucharistic teaching, they replied, 'To *whom* shall we go?' Not,
'*Where* shall we go?' They understood no more about the
Eucharist than did the five thousand minus twelve who
departed; but they understood very clearly that without Jesus
they were nowhere. If accepting his teaching was a condition of
staying with him, they accepted his teaching. There is another
delightful irony. 'To whom shall we go?' implies, 'If there were
anywhere else, or anyone else, to go to, we *would* go! You're
stuck with us!' This artlessness is of course a beautiful compli-
ment to Jesus, an impulsive recognition of total trust, not in his
teaching, but in him.

In our lives too we must ask, not '*What* is the meaning to life?' but '*Who* is the meaning to life?' And as people alone give our lives meaning, why not follow such an instinct in prayer?